Growing Your Vocabulary:

Learning from Latin and Greek Roots

Level 6

Prestwick House

Senior Editor:
Paul Moliken

Editors:
Darlene Gilmore
Elizabeth Osborne
Stephanie Polukis
Daniel Reed
Magedah Shabo
Sally Wein

Cover and Text Design:
Larry Knox

Illustrator:
Ned Harrison

Layout and Production:
Jeremy Clark

Prestwick House

ISBN: 978-158049-872-2

Contents

Growing Your Vocabulary: Learning from Latin and Greek Roots

3

Growing Your Vocabulary: Learning from Latin and Greek Roots

Introduction

To Students

Honor, honorable, honor roll, honorary. What do all these words have in common? *Honor*, of course! Because you already know that honor has to do with respect or special recognition, you can give some meaning to all of the words. Fluent readers have learned to break words into parts and then put the parts back together. By understanding parts of words, you can figure out the meanings of whole words.

Learning Latin and Greek roots will help you figure out the meanings of many words in the English language. For example, the root *viv* means "to live." You probably already know that *survive* means "to stay alive." But, did you know that *vivid* means "lifelike"? The root *dict* means "to say, speak." Do you think the words *predict* and *dictate* might have something to do with speaking?

As you begin to recognize Latin and Greek roots in unfamiliar words, you can ask yourself if the root's meaning makes sense in the context.

The goal of using this book is to have fun with words while you increase vocabulary and word recognition.

Getting Started

The 20 chapters in this book are based on themes. For example, Chapter 4 is all about light, while Chapter 10 is all about human beings.

In each chapter, you will learn two to four roots and up to ten vocabulary words. The first two to four pages are instruction. This text provides meanings and origins of the roots, as well as the definitions of the vocabulary words. It also includes information about each of the words.

The last few pages of each chapter are exercises to practice what you've learned. There are matching activities, games, and creative writing prompts—something for everyone. And to keep all these roots and vocabulary words fresh in your mind, be sure to complete the review exercise after every five chapters.

Good luck growing your vocabulary!

Progeny

Congenital

Gene

Generate

Genre

Generic

Growing Your Vocabulary: Learning from Latin and Greek Roots

gener

gen

Chapter 1:

It's in the Genes

Many of the words you are going to learn in this chapter are words that you may have heard in science class. This chapter is all about words that have to do with birth, creation, kind, and type.

Roots to Learn:	Words to Learn:	Prefix:	Suffixes:
gen gener	gene generate congenital genre progeny generic	pro–	–al –ic/ics –ate

The Greek noun **GENOS** means "family." The Latin verb **GIGNERE, GENITUS** means "to give birth" or "create."

noun

A **GENE** is a biological unit of material passed from parent to child that determines which traits the child will inherit.

Scientists do not know how many genes are in the average human body. They estimate that there are around 70,000! That's an awful lot to count and keep track of!

*Scientists have discovered a **gene** that contributes to obesity.*

SUFFIX ALARM!
The suffix –ic or –ics means "having the quality or nature of something."
Examples: metal + –ic = metallic—made of or like metal
hero + –ic = heroic—having qualities of a hero

Growing Your Vocabulary: Learning from Latin and Greek Roots

Chapter 1:
It's in the Genes

adjective

CONGENITAL means "occurring at birth" and is often used to describe medical conditions. You may have heard the term "congenital birth defect" or "congenital heart disease."

Many congenital problems, which used to cause serious health issues later in life, can now be treated before a baby is born.

*White cats are more likely to have **congenital** deafness.*

SUFFIX ALARM!
The suffix –al means "having the quality or physical makeup of something."
Examples: accident + –al = accidental—happening by chance
alphabetic + –al = alphabetical—arranged in the order of the alphabet

---

*The **progeny** of the champion racehorse went on to win many awards.*

noun **PROGENY** are the offspring of living organisms.

One of the basic needs of all living things, both plants and animals, is to reproduce.

PREFIX ALARM!
The prefix *pro–* has several meanings. One definition is "forward" or "before."
Example:
pro– + active = proactive—ready to take action before an event occurs

Finally, the Latin **GENUS**, **GENERIS** means "race" or "type." The root of this word, **GENER**, is found in many words dealing with both family and kind or type.

GENERATE means "to bring into existence" or "to make happen." When you create or build something, you generate it. You can even generate writing or ideas!

verb

*The magnet **generates** a a force field that can attract some metallic objects.*

> ## SUFFIX ALARM!
> The suffix *–ate* is used to make a verb out of a noun and means "to cause to be" or "to make."
> *Example: hyphen + –ate = hyphenate – to create a new word by joining two separate words with a dash*

GENRE means "type," "class," or "category."

~~adj~~ noun

*The judges could not decide what **genre** the writer's work belonged to.*

GENERIC means "like all the others in a category or class."

adjective

GENERIC also has a special meaning when it comes to things that we buy. It refers to products that do not have recognizable brand names. Somebody who wants to save money might buy a generic cereal instead.

MARY BROWN WENT TO THE MALL AND BOUGHT SOME BEACH TOWELS FOR HER FRIEND BOB SMITH. THE END

*Jorge used very **generic** names for the people and places in his story.*

Exercises
Word Bank

gene	progeny	genre
congenital	generate	generic

I. Define It! (Part I) *do*

DIRECTIONS: Write the letter of the word from the right column that matches the definition in the left column. The first one has been done for you.

1. of no particular kind or type **C**
2. type; class; category *e*
3. the offspring of living organisms *a*
4. biological material passed from parent to child that determines which traits a child will inherit *d*
5. to create *f*
6. occurring at birth *b*

A. progeny
B. congenital
C. generic
D. gene
E. genre
F. generate

II. Finish It! *do*

DIRECTIONS: Using the root, write a word to complete each sentence.
The first one has been done for you.

1. It is likely that the winner of the American Kennel Dog Show will be the ____**progeny**____ of a former champion. (Root = GEN)
2. When writing an essay, a student should be able to *generate* more than one or two paragraphs. (Root = GENER)
3. To save money at the grocery store, my mother likes to buy the *generic* brands of cereal rather than Frosted Fruit because they are usually less expensive. (Root = GENER)
4. Susie has brown eyes because she received a dominant *gene* for them from both of her parents. (Root = GEN)
5. In literature class, students study many different *genre* of writing, such as poetry, nonfiction, drama, novels, and short stories. (Root = GENER)
6. The prize cow had a calf with five legs, which is a serious *congenital* birth defect. (Root = GEN)

························· *Word Bank* ·························

gene   progeny   genre
congenital   generate   generic

III. Define It! (Part 2)

DIRECTIONS: Based on what you have learned in this chapter, define each of the following in your own words, and create a sentence using the word.

1. gene: _____

_____

2. congenital: _____

_____

3. progeny: _____

_____

4. generate: _____

_____

5. genre: _____

_____

6. generic: _____

_____

IV. Personalize It!

DIRECTIONS: Using your understanding of the vocabulary words, respond to the following prompts. Use a separate piece of paper, if necessary.

1. Which literary *genres* have you had the opportunity to read? Which is your favorite *genre*, and what is the name of your favorite piece in that *genre*? Why do you like it better than other types of writing?

_____

2. Use some *generic* adjectives to describe a movie (for example, *nice*). Then use some specific adjectives (for example, *thrilling*). How are the two kinds of adjectives different?

_____

3. If you could inherit a *gene* from anyone in the world, what would it be and from whom would you like to inherit it?

_____

4. What characteristic do you have that you hope to pass on to your *progeny*? Why?

_____

··················· *Word Bank* ···················

gene   progeny   genre
congenital   generate   generic

V. Decode It!

DIRECTIONS: Use what you have learned about the roots *gen* and *gener* and the prefixes and suffixes in this chapter to answer the following questions:

1. The Latin prefix *re–* means "again." Review the definition of the root *gener*. What do you think *regenerate* means?

   _____

2. The prefix *de–* means "down" or "opposite of." What do you think *degenerate* means?

   _____

3. When a person is born, he or she has certain physical characteristics that others can see. These characteristics are called phenotypes. Phenotypes and *genotypes* are related. What do you think a *genotype* is?

   _____

4. The Latin verb *gignere, genitus* means "to give birth" or "create." The first book of the Bible is called *Genesis*. Why do you think this name is used for the first book?

   _____

VI. Put It In Context!

DIRECTIONS: For each vocabulary word, write a detailed sentence that explains the meaning of the word through the context of the sentence. You may change the part of speech to fit your sentences.

1. generic: *The non-spesific type of thing.*

2. genre: *The type or class someone or something is in.*

3. generate: *Something you can make or create.*

4. progeny: *The kids of a couple.*

5. congenital: *Something that occures at birth*

6. gene: *Something that can determine your physical feetures*

Growing Your Vocabulary: Learning from Latin and Greek Roots

VII. Solve It!

DIRECTIONS: Use the clues and words from this chapter to complete the crossword puzzle. Some of the words may be in a different part of speech.

Word Bank

- genes
- congenital
- progeny
- generated
- genres
- generic

[crossword puzzle filled in:]

1 (across): c o n g e n I t a l
2 (down): n e a t i c s / g e n e r i c s
3 (across): g e n e r a t e d
4 (across): p r o g e n y
5 (down): g e n e s
6 (across): g e n r e s

oeanitegrn

~~generation~~

Clues:

ACROSS

1. inherited; present from birth

3. The candles _____ just enough light for us when the power went out.

4. These names are placed on the leaves of a family tree.

6. short story, novel, play, lyric poem, limerick, and haiku

DOWN

2. This type of product is often cheaper and has a simpler label or design than a name brand.

5. These can determine your physical features, such as height and eye color.

Unscramble the letters in the circles in the crossword puzzle to make a word that fits in the blank in the sentence below. The unscrambled word is not one of the vocabulary words from this lesson, but it is related to some of them.

Your parents and grandparents are not from the same _____ as you.

generation

······················· *Word Bank* ·······················

gene	progeny	genre
congenital	generate	generic

VIII. Write About It!

DIRECTIONS: In this chapter, you have learned words about birth, creation, and type. Think about the characteristics that make you who you are. Do you think that the kind of person you are is determined mostly by your genes or by your experiences? Do you think that your most important qualities are set at birth, or do you think that the choices you make really say more about you? Explain your answers.

_____

_____

_____

_____

_____

_____

_____

_____

_____

_____

Survive

Vivacious

Revive

Vivid

Immortal

Mortal

Morbid

Mortify

Growing Your Vocabulary: Learning from Latin and Greek Roots

mort

mor

viv

Chapter 2:
A Matter of Life and Death

Mahatma Gandhi, an inspiring leader who dedicated his life to serving people and taught the importance of honesty and nonviolence, once said, "Live as if you were to die tomorrow. Learn as if you were to live forever." In this chapter, you'll learn words that are related to living and dying—the very concepts that Gandhi spoke about.

Roots to Learn:	**Words to Learn:**	**Prefixes:**	**Suffixes:**
viv mort/mor	survive mortal revive immortal vivid mortify vivacious morbid	re– im–	–ious –ify

The Latin word **VIVERE** means "to live." The root **VIV** comes from the word **VIVERE**. From this root, we get the following words:

SURVIVE means "to live through." *verb*

Many people **SURVIVE** a dangerous situation like a hurricane, tornado, or an accident simply by remaining calm and waiting for help to arrive. The worst thing you can do is panic.

verb

REVIVE means "to bring back to life."

Modern medicine has become so advanced that many people who, in the past, would have died from a disease or an operation have been **REVIVED**.

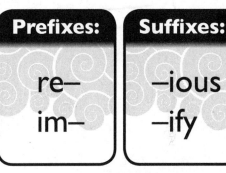

*The hiker **survived** the avalanche by digging a small breathing hole in the snow.*

Doctors use various modern techniques, such as electrically shocking the heart or performing CPR, to revive people whose hearts have stopped.

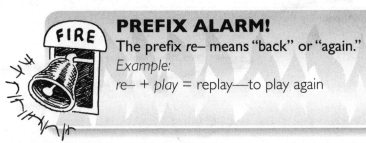

PREFIX ALARM!
The prefix *re–* means "back" or "again."
Example:
re– + *play* = replay—to play again

Chapter 2:
A Matter of Life and Death

VIVID means "lifelike." *ad.*

Some movies that use computer generated animation are so **VIVID** that people in the audience can't tell if the actors or the special effects are real or not.

Have you ever had a dream so vivid that when you woke up you thought it was real?

*The memory of the carnival was still **vivid** in Samira's mind months later.*

ad.

We get the word **VIVACIOUS** from the root **VIV**. **VIVACIOUS** means "lively in temper or spirit." You can think of it as "full of life."

SUFFIX ALARM!
The suffix *–ious* means "full of." This suffix changes the ending of a word in different ways.
Examples: anxiety – iety + –ious = anxious—full of anxiety
nutrition – ion + –ious = nutritious—full of nutrition

Growing Your Vocabulary: Learning from Latin and Greek Roots

The Latin noun **MORS, MORTIS** means "death."
We get the roots **MOR** and **MORT** from this word.

ad.

MORTAL beings will eventually die. All living things on Earth are **MORTAL**.

The oldest tree that is still living is more than 4,600 years old! That means the tree is as old as the Pyramids in Egypt. It is called a bristlecone pine tree, and it is located in the Rocky Mountains. Even though it is that old, it will eventually die because it is mortal.

*While Marilyn Monroe's films will continue to be watched forever, she, unfortunately, was **mortal**.*

PREFIX ALARM!
The prefix im– means "not." Im– is a version of the prefix in–, which also means "not."
Example:
im– + proper = improper—not right

ad.

IMMORTAL beings will never die. Although Marilyn Monroe died in 1962, she remains **IMMORTAL** on film.

*Zeus is the **immortal** king of the Greek gods.*

"Every man dies—Not every man really lives."
—WILLIAM ROSS WALLACE

Chapter 2:
A Matter of Life and Death

verb

To **MORTIFY** is to embarrass someone so much that he or she wishes to die.

You will probably be **MORTIFIED** if your biggest secret is spread all over school.

*Alice was **mortified** when her notes blew off the stage in the middle of her presentation.*

SUFFIX ALARM!

The suffix –ify means "to cause."
Example:
null + –*ify* = nullify—to cause something to be unimportant or worthless

*Toni's father said her fascination with graveyards was **morbid**.*

ad.

MORBID means "sick" or "unhealthy" (especially in thought or desire).

Much of Gothic literature centers on **MORBID** subjects such as death, horror, or pain. Edgar Allan Poe is a Gothic writer, although he did not invent the literary genre. Can you think of any other authors you have read who would be considered Gothic writers?

Growing Your Vocabulary: Learning from Latin and Greek Roots

Exercises
Word Bank

revive	vivid	mortal	mortify
survive	vivacious	immortal	morbid

I. Define It! (Part 1)

DIRECTIONS: Write the letter of the word from the right column that matches the definition in the left column. The first one has been done for you.

1. full of life **F**
2. not living forever; able to die _B_
3. to bring back to life _G_
4. sick or unhealthy (especially in thought or desire) _A_
5. to embarrass someone so much that he or she wishes to die _H_
6. lifelike _E_
7. to live through _D_
8. never dying _C_

A. morbid
B. mortal
C. immortal
D. survive
E. vivid
F. vivacious
G. revive
H. mortify

II. Finish It!

DIRECTIONS: Using the root, write a word to complete each sentence.
The first one has been done for you.

1. Many people would have a difficult time trying to _____**survive**_____ on an island without food or water. (Root = VIV)
2. The DJ played some dance music in order to ___vivid___ the dull, lifeless party. (Root = VIV) [revive written above]
3. The ___vivacious___ cheerleaders performed an energetic routine, even though their team was losing badly. (Root = VIV)
4. When Ms. Banks made Keith read aloud a note he was passing during class, he was ___mortified___ because the note was very personal. (Root = MORT)
5. Could you imagine how crowded the world would be if everyone were ___immortal___ and no one died? (Root = MORT)
6. Tristan's parents thought he was ___morbid___ because he liked to dress up as a scary monster. (Root = MOR)
7. The kindergarten teacher wore ___vivid___ clothes of green, orange, and yellow, and decorated her classroom in bright and sunny colors. (Root = VIV)
8. In many cartoons, the characters do not seem to be ___immortal___ [mortal written above]; they can survive exploding bombs, anvils falling from the sky, and falls from high places. (Root = MORT)

·· *Word Bank* ··

revive	vivid	mortal	mortify
survive	vivacious	immortal	morbid

III. Define It! (Part 2)

DIRECTIONS: Based on what you have learned in this chapter, define each of the following in your own words, and create a sentence using the word.

1. mortify: _____
_____

2. immortal: _____
_____

3. morbid: _____
_____

4. mortal: _____
_____

5. revive: _____
_____

6. survive: _____
_____

7. vivid: _____
_____

8. vivacious: _____
_____

IV. Personalize It!

DIRECTIONS: Using your understanding of the vocabulary words, respond to the following prompts. Use a separate piece of paper, if necessary.

1. Describe the most *vivid* memory that you have. What makes it so realistic or memorable?
_____

2. How would being *immortal* change the way you do things every day?
_____

3. Describe how you would *survive* if you had to live in Antarctica.
_____

4. Describe a *morbid* movie you have seen or book you have read. Describe how it made you feel.
_____

5. If you are at a party, and someone says the host is *convivial*, what type of person is being described? What other words might you use to describe the person?
_____

Growing Your Vocabulary: Learning from Latin and Greek Roots

Word Bank

revive	vivid	mortal	mortify
survive	vivacious	immortal	morbid

V. Compare It!

DIRECTIONS: In this chapter, two of the words are antonyms. *Immortal* means "never dying," and *mortal* means "able to die." For each of the vocabulary words in the chapter, find an antonym and then use the antonym correctly in a sentence.

1. mortify:

_____

2. morbid:

_____

3. revive:

_____

4. survive:

_____

5. vivid:

_____

6. vivacious:

_____

VI. Put It In Context!

DIRECTIONS: For each vocabulary word, write a detailed sentence that explains the meaning of the word through the context of the sentence. You may change the part of speech to fit your sentences.

1. immortal: all The Greek and Roman Gods are immortal, they can't die.

2. mortal: I am mortal. I will die soon.

3. mortify: I was morified when I pooped on my first day of school.

4. vivacious: I was vivacious when I was jumping around like crazy.

5. morbid: When you are dying you are morbid.

6. revive: To revive is to bring back to life.

7. survive: I survived DC superheroes rolling over me.

8. vivid: You were vidid and bright.

Chapter 2:
Exercises

VII. Solve It!

DIRECTIONS: Use the clues and words from this chapter to complete the crossword puzzle. Some of the words may be in a different part of speech.

Word Bank

revive
survivor
vivid
vivacious
mortal
immortal
mortified
morbid

miiocatr

Clues:

ACROSS

4. The works of Edgar Allan Poe are Gothic, which often is about __morbid__ subjects.

6. The painting of the sunset was so __vivid__ that I thought it was a photograph.

7. The explorer Juan Ponce de León searched for a magical fountain that would make him __immortal__ so he would never die.

8. John Krakauer wrote a book called *Into Thin Air* about his experience of being stranded on a mountain; he is an example of a __survivor__.

DOWN

1. A person learns CPR so he or she will be able to __revive__ someone.

2. If I gave a speech in front of a large group of people and forgot a few lines, I would feel __mortified__.

3. The __vivacious__ meerkats scampered around their den with intense energy.

5. Humans are __mortal__, the opposite of Greek gods like Apollo.

Unscramble the letters in the circles in the crossword puzzle to make a word that answers the riddle below. The unscrambled word is not one of the vocabulary words from this lesson, but it is related to some of them.

I am a person who is in charge of a body before a funeral. __MORTICIAN__

-------- *Word Bank* --------

revive	vivid	mortal	mortify
survive	vivacious	immortal	morbid

VIII. Write About It!

DIRECTIONS: In this chapter, you have learned words about living and dying. An *obituary* is a genre of writing that gives notice about a person's death and includes a short description of the person's life. The word *obituary* comes from the Latin word *obitus* meaning "death."

Read the example obituaries your teacher has provided. Then, write an obituary for yourself. Use at least three words from the word bank.

_____

_____

_____

_____

_____

_____

_____

_____

_____

_____

Cardiologist

Hemorrhage   Neonatal

Cardiovascular

Epidermis

Prenatal

Dermatology

Anemia

Growing Your Vocabulary: Learning from Latin and Greek Roots

derm

card

nat

hem/em

Chapter 3:

Skin, Blood, and Other Things

Does the title of the chapter disturb you? This chapter isn't as gross as it may seem. It's all about words that are used to describe things that have to do with your body.

Roots to Learn:	**Words to Learn:**	**Prefixes:**	**Suffixes:**
card derm hem/em nat	cardiologist anemia cardiovascular hemorrhage epidermis prenatal dermatology neonatal	cardio– pre– epi– neo– a–	–logy –ist

The Greek word **KARDIA** means "heart." From its root **CARD**, we get words with the prefix *cardio–*.

A **CARDIOLOGIST** is someone who studies the heart.

This type of doctor uses instruments that show how a person's heart works. From the results, the doctor can then prescribe the right treatment if something is actually wrong.

CARDIOVASCULAR relates to the network by which the heart transports blood throughout the body.

*Mark's **cardiologist** gave him some blunt advice: get some exercise or risk a heart attack.*

SUFFIX ALARM!
The suffix *–ist* means "one who studies something."
Examples:
biology – *y* + *–ist* = biologist—a person who studies biology
cartoon + *–ist* = cartoonist—a person who works with cartoons

Growing Your Vocabulary: Learning from Latin and Greek Roots

Chapter 3:
Skin, Blood, and Other Things

The Greek word **DERMA** means "skin"; its root **DERM** gives us the following words:

The **EPIDERMIS** is the outside layer of skin.

Did You Know?

One main job of the epidermis, surprisingly, is to act as waterproofing for a person's body. Every minute you lose 30,000 cells from your epidermis, so it may be thin, but there's a lot of it!

AH, SMELL THAT FRESH AIR!

*Since the earthworm breathes through its skin, its **epidermis** must be thin enough to let oxygen pass through.*

PREFIX ALARM!

FIRE

The prefix *epi–* means "on," "beside," "after," or "around."
Example:
epi– + *demic* = epidemic—something, usually a disease, that affects a large number of people

---

SUN-BLAST TANNING LOTION

OUCH!

*Research about **dermatology** has uncovered a link between tanning and skin cancer.*

DERMATOLOGY is the study of the skin.

A dermatologist is a doctor who deals with diseases of the skin, such as acne or warts.

noun

SUFFIX ALARM!

FIRE

The suffix *–logy* means "the study of" or "the science of."
Examples:
volcano + *–logy* = volcanology—the study of volcanoes
zoo + *–logy* = zoology—the study of animals

Growing Your Vocabulary: Learning from Latin and Greek Roots

The Greek word for "blood" is **HAIMA**. Its roots are **HEM** and **EM**.

ANEMIA is a lack of red blood cells, or hemoglobin, that should be inside them.

Did You Know?

There are several types of anemia. The most common is "iron-deficiency anemia," in which a person does not get enough iron from food. In "sickle-cell anemia," however, the red blood cells are misshapen. They cannot move easily through blood vessels because of their shape. If blood cannot move to all parts of the body, cells cannot get the oxygen they need to function. Anemia can also be caused by blood loss.

HEALTHY CELLS MOVE FREELY.

SICKLED CELLS JAM EASILY.

 FIRE

PREFIX ALARM!

The prefix *a–* or *an–* means "without."
Examples:
a– + *typical* = atypical—out of the ordinary; not normal
an– + *aerobic* = anaerobic—without air

To **HEMORRHAGE** is to bleed excessively.

When a major blood vessel or artery is cut, a **HEMORRHAGE** can occur. Minor cuts do not cause this. The human body contains about 5 quarts of blood, so small cuts that don't blled much do not cause serious damage.

NO MORE PORCUPINE JUGGLING, OKAY?

*The woman's leg was **hemorrhaging**. The doctor elevated her leg and applied a bandage.*

Chapter 3:
Skin, Blood, and Other Things

The Latin word **NATUS**, which includes the root **NAT**, means "born."

PRENATAL means "occurring before birth."

To have a healthy baby, mothers need to be careful about many things, like eating the right foods, not smoking or drinking, and getting enough rest.

*Folic acid is important to **prenatal** health.*

PREFIX ALARM!
The prefix *pre–* means "before in time, place, or order of importance."
Examples: pre– + *view* = preview—viewing ahead of time
pre– + *teen* = preteen—before the age of thirteen

*The **neonatal** unit in a hospital takes care of infants who are born prematurely.*

NEONATAL means "having to do with newborns."

Did You Know?
Almost half a million babies are born prematurely each year. The record for early birth weight belongs to a baby born in 2004—she weighed only 8.6 ounces, less than a glass of water, and was only 8 inches long. Thanks to good neonatal care, she is fine today.

PREFIX ALARM!
The prefix *neo–* means "new."
Example:
neo– + *classical* = neoclassical—a revival of the classical period in literature and art

Growing Your Vocabulary: Learning from Latin and Greek Roots

Exercises
Word Bank

cardiologist   epidermis   anemia   prenatal
cardiovascular dermatology hemorrhage neonatal

I. Define It! (Part I)

DIRECTIONS: Write the letter of the word from the right column that matches the definition in the left column. The first one has been done for you.

1. the study of the skin **C**
2. a great flow of blood outward B
3. the outside layer of the skin F
4. occurring before birth A
5. relating to the body system that contains the heart and blood H
6. having to do with newborns G
7. someone who studies the heart E
8. a lack of iron in the blood anemia D

A. prenatal
B. hemorrhage
C. dermatology
D. anemia
E. cardiologist
F. epidermis
G. neonatal
H. cardiovascular

II. Finish It!

DIRECTIONS: Using the root, write a word to complete each sentence. The first one has been done for you.

1. **Anemia** is a potentially dangerous medical condition that causes a person to feel unusually tired. (Root = EM)
2. When Captain Jacques-Yves Cousteau went diving underneath the continent of Antarctica, he needed to protect his _epidermis_ from frostbite. (Root = DERM)
3. A person who begins to _hemorrhage_ will need a transfusion to replace the lost blood. (Root = HEM)
4. Only newborn babies are treated in the _neonatal_ wing of the hospital. (Root = NAT)
5. When my grandfather had a heart attack, he had to visit a(n) _cardiologist_ for treatment. (Root = CARD)
6. Many pregnant women get _prenatal_ care, such as blood tests and regular checkups to monitor the baby's growth. (Root = NAT)
7. Acne, hives, rashes, and eczema are some of the skin diseases you learn about if you study _dermatology_. (Root = DERM)
8. Jumping rope is an excellent way to improve your _cardiovascular_ system because the exercising makes your heart stronger. (Root = CARD)

Chapter 3:
Exercises

.... *Word Bank* ....

| cardiologist | epidermis | anemia | prenatal |
| cardiovascular | dermatology | hemorrhage | neonatal |

III. Define It! (Part 2)

DIRECTIONS: Based on what you have learned in this chapter, define each of the following in your own words, and create a sentence using the word.

1. cardiologist: _____

_____

2. cardiovascular: _____

_____

3. dermatology: _____

_____

4. epidermis: _____

_____

5. anemia: _____

_____

6. hemorrhage: _____

_____

7. prenatal: _____

_____

8. neonatal: _____

_____

IV. Decode It!

DIRECTIONS: Use what you have learned about the roots *card*, *derma*, *hem*, *em*, and *nat* and the prefixes and suffixes in this chapter to answer the following questions:

1. Review the suffix *–ology* and the root word for blood. What do you think *hematology* is?

_____

2. The suffix *–ist* means "one who studies or supports something." What word is the name for a person who practices pacifism or nonviolence?

_____

3. The suffix *–stasis* means "a stopping of." In this chapter, you learned that the word *haima* means "blood." What do you think the medical term *hemostasis* means?

_____

4. The Greek root *pathos* means "emotion." In this chapter you learned that *a–* or *an–* means "without." What type of person is an *apathetic* person? What other words might you use to describe the person?

_____

Growing Your Vocabulary: Learning from Latin and Greek Roots

.... *Word Bank* ....

cardiologist	epidermis	anemia	prenatal
cardiovascular	dermatology	hemorrhage	neonatal

V. Analogies!

DIRECTIONS: For each of the vocabulary words in the chapter, complete the analogy.

1. *Geology* is to *geologist* as *cardiology* is to _____.

2. *Midnight* is to *noon* as *born* is to _____.

3. *Lack of sleep* is to *fatigue* as *lack of iron* is to _____.

4. *Neurology* is to *the nervous system* as *cardiology* is to *the* _____ *system.*

5. *Topsoil* is to *Earth* as the _____ is to *the body.*

6. *Tears* is to *cry* as *blood* is to _____.

7. *Animals* is to *zoology* as *skin* is to _____.

8. *Preschool* is to *elementary school* as *prenatal* is to _____.

VI. Put It In Context!

DIRECTIONS: For each vocabulary word, write a detailed sentence that explains the meaning of the word through the context of the sentence. You may change the part of speech to fit your sentences.

1. cardiovascular:

_____

2. epidermis:

_____

3. prenatal:

_____

4. dermatologist:

_____

5. neonatal:

_____

6. hemorrhage:

_____

7. anemia:

_____

8. cardiologist:

_____

Chapter 3:
Exercises

VII. Solve It!

DIRECTIONS: Use the clues and words from this chapter to complete the crossword puzzle. Some of the words may be a different part of speech.

Word Bank

- cardiologist
- cardiovascular
- epidermis
- dermatology
- anemia
- hemorrhage
- prenatal
- neonatal

mohnepceil

Clues:

ACROSS

3. A pamphlet that explains healthful habits for a mother during her pregnancy would be used for what type of care?

6. This person is a doctor who specializes in the heart.

7. If you have poor blood circulation, your doctor may look at this body system.

8. Someone studying this medical field would look at skin diseases and burns.

DOWN

1. If this starts to happen to you, go to the hospital right away.

2. A doctor would perform this type of exam at a baby's first check-up.

4. A person who suffers from this condition may feel unusually tired all the time.

5. In the summer, we protect this by wearing sunscreen.

Unscramble the letters in the circles in the crossword puzzle to make a word that fits in the blank in the sentence below. The unscrambled word is not one of the vocabulary words from this lesson, but it is related to some of them.

A disease that prevents blood from clotting. __ __ __ __ __ __ __ __ __ . __ __

Word Bank

cardiologist	epidermis	anemia	prenatal
cardiovascular	dermatology	hemorrhage	neonatal

VIII. Write About It!

DIRECTIONS: Two of the words in this chapter have to do with the heart. Write a paragraph about what you can do to keep your heart healthy and strong. Try to use at least three words from this chapter.

_____

_____

_____

_____

_____

_____

_____

_____

_____

Photosynthesis

Elucidate

Illuminate

Lucid

Luminary

Luminous

Photon

Growing Your Vocabulary: Learning from Latin and Greek Roots

lumin

phot luc

Chapter 4:

Light and its Travels

Did you know that the speed of light is 299,792,458 meters per second, which is also 186,282 miles per second? This chapter is all about words that have to do with light and its travels.

Roots to Learn:

lumin   phot

luc

Words to Learn:

luminous   elucidate
luminary   photon
illuminate   photosynthesis
lucid

Suffix:

–er

The Latin word **LUMEN, LUMINIS** means "light." The root **LUMIN** comes from this noun.

adjective

LUMINOUS means "filled with light."

Often, the moon appears **LUMINOUS**, but it shines only because it reflects the sun's light.

noun

A **LUMINARY** is a person who is very inspiring or influential. A **LUMINARY** is also an object that gives off light.

verb

ILLUMINATE means "to light up." Many people have a floodlight that will **ILLUMINATE** their driveway at night.

*The townspeople reported seeing a **luminous** saucer that they believed to be a UFO.*

SUFFIX ALARM!
The suffix –er means "one who."
Examples:
lead + –er = leader—one who leads
sing + –er = singer—one who sings

Chapter 4:
Light and its Travels

The Latin word **LUX, LUCIS** also means "light." It gives us the root **LUC**.

LUCID means "clear" or "able to be understood."

To make glass clear, or **LUCID**, companies use sand, similar to sand on beaches. But how can this be made so you can see through it? First of all, sand is separated into regular and "quartz sand," which is pure. Then, the quartz sand is heated, cooled very quickly, and poured into the right shape. This process makes the glass clear.

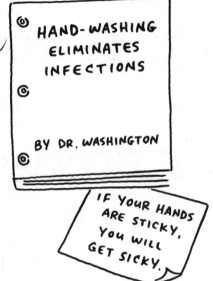

adjective

HAND-WASHING
ELIMINATES
INFECTIONS

BY DR. WASHINGTON

IF YOUR HANDS
ARE STICKY,
YOU WILL
GET SICKY.

*The doctor wrote a **lucid** article about the link between hand-washing and infection.*

FRESH DOUGH.

HOLD THE ANCHOVIES.

MAKE IT ROUND.

LOTS OF CHEESE.

*Mario can describe and **elucidate** all the qualities of a perfect pizza.*

ELUCIDATE means "to make clear."

verb (verbs)

Sometimes, a subject in school isn't quite clear to you. You need your teacher or someone else to explain it further so you can understand it better. The person, obviously, is to **ELUCIDATE** it for you.

You can easily see the relationship between *lucid* and *elucidate*. They both have to do with clearing something up. Remember, many words that include *luc* deal with light. Light can make things clear.

The Greek noun that means "light" is **PHOS, PHOTOS**. We get the root **PHOT** from this word.

A **PHOTON** is a particle that carries electromagnetic energy such as light.

noun

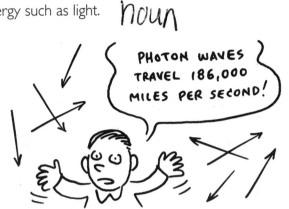

PHOTON WAVES TRAVEL 186,000 MILES PER SECOND!

The energy that is used in a microwave to heat food is carried by **PHOTONS**. X-rays are made up of photons that carry a lot of energy and are used by doctors to create images of our bones. Gamma rays, which are harnessed to fight cancer cells, are also photons. Although we cannot see individual photons, we can see the many effects they have in our everyday lives.

*A **photon** has no mass and no electric charge.*

Did You Know?
Gamma ray bursts from outside the Milky Way galaxy have been known to release more energy in 10 seconds than our Sun will in its entire lifetime!

PHOTOSYNTHESIS is the process by which plants use light to make food. *noun*

The word **PHOTOSYNTHESIS** is formed from two root words. The first is the Greek word *photos*. The second is also a Greek word; *synthesis* means "to put together."

*All plants need sunlight to begin the process of **photosynthesis**.*

Growing Your Vocabulary: Learning from Latin and Greek Roots

Chapter 4:
Light and its Travels
Exercises
Word Bank

| luminous | illuminate | elucidate | photosynthesis |
| luminary | lucid | photon | |

I. Define It! (Part 1)

DIRECTIONS: Write the letter of the word from the right column that matches the definition in the left column. The first one has been done for you.

1. filled with light **B**
2. clear or able to be understood *G*
3. a particle of energy that may also travel as light *a*
4. a person who is said to be very wise or enlightened *e*
5. the process by which plants use light to make food *d*
6. to make clear *f*
7. to light up *C*

A. photon
B. luminous
C. illuminate
D. photosynthesis
E. luminary
F. elucidate
G. lucid

II. Select It!

DIRECTIONS: Using the root, write a word to complete each sentence. The first one has been done for you.

1. The instructions to install the DVD player were so _____**lucid**_____ that Tom was able to connect it to the television without making any mistakes. (Root = LUC)
2. Lisa asked the teacher to repeat and _____*elucidate*_____ the directions because they were difficult to understand. (Root = LUC)
3. Some fish are able to _____*illuminate*_____ themselves at will; they use their light to attract prey. (Root = LUMIN)
4. Although individual _____*Photons*_____ cannot be seen, they certainly have important functions. (Root = PHOT)
5. There is little chance for _____*photosynthesis*_____ in my shady backyard; nothing seems to grow there. (Root = PHOT)
6. Some gardeners install lights around their gardens in order to create a(n) _____*luminous*_____ landscape. (Root = LUMIN)
7. I made my own _____*luminary*_____ by putting a candle in a brown paper bag with sand in the bottom. (Root = LUMIN)

40

Growing Your Vocabulary: Learning from Latin and Greek Roots

··· *Word Bank* ···

luminous   illuminate   elucidate   photosynthesis
luminary   lucid   photon

III. Define It! (Part 2)

DIRECTIONS: Based on what you have learned in this chapter, define each of the following in your own words, and create a sentence using the word.

1. luminous: _____
_____

2. luminary: _____
_____

3. illuminate: _____
_____

4. lucid: _____
_____

5. elucidate: _____
_____

6. photon: _____
_____

7. photosynthesis: _____
_____

IV. Personalize It!

DIRECTIONS: Using your understanding of the vocabulary words, respond to the following prompts.

1. Sometimes the directions for an assignment may be unclear. What are four questions you might ask if you want a teacher to *elucidate* an assignment?
_____
_____

2. We are all experts in something. You might understand how to work with wood, or you might understand the rules of a game that confuse others. Give a *lucid* explanation of something that may seem complicated to others.
_____
_____

3. Let's suppose that there is a storm in your town, and all the power goes out. Describe four ways to *illuminate* your home so you and others can see.
_____
_____

4. We all know of someone who could be considered an expert in a certain area. For example, Alexander Graham Bell was a *luminary* in the field of electronics. Write about someone you think could be considered a *luminary*, and explain your answer.
_____
_____

.... Word Bank ....

luminous	illuminate	elucidate	photosynthesis
luminary	lucid	photon	

V. Decode It!

DIRECTIONS: Use what you have learned about the roots *lumin*, *luc*, and *phot* in this chapter to answer the following questions:

1. *Sensitive* means "highly responsive" or "easily hurt or damaged." What do you think *photosensitive* means?

   _____

2. The prefix *trans–* means "beyond." The Latin word *lucere* means "to shine." What do you think a *translucent* object looks like?

   _____

3. The suffix *–ity* means "state of." What do you think *luminosity* means?

   _____

4. The word *bioluminescent* includes the Greek root *bio* meaning "life." One meaning of the suffix *–escent* is "able to give off light." What do you think is special about a *bioluminescent* organism?

   _____

VI. Compare It!

DIRECTIONS: An *antonym* is a word that means the opposite. For example, the antonym of the word *translucent*, which means "able to be seen through," is *opaque*. Match each of the following vocabulary words to its antonym. Then, match the vocabulary word with its synonym.

Antonyms	Vocabulary Word	Synonyms
A. baffling	1. luminous	F. a wise person
B. darken	2. elucidate	G. reveal
C. confuse	3. lucid	H. radiant
D. dull	4. luminary	I. light up
E. a nobody	5. illuminate	J. clear

·················· *Word Bank* ··················

| luminous | illuminate | elucidate | photosynthesis |
| luminary | lucid | photon | |

VII. Unscramble It!

DIRECTIONS: The vocabulary words from the chapter have been scrambled. Using the sentence, figure out which word belongs in the blank. Then, unscramble the letters to write the word correctly.

1. The directions for putting together the bicycle were so ___lucid___ that Rudolph was able to
   CUILD
   assemble it in less than an hour. ✓

2. Solar panels use the energy in ___photons___ of sunlight to produce electricity. ✓
   SOPHNTO

3. Our sixteenth president, Abraham Lincoln, was said to be a ___luminary___ because of his vast
   RILNYUMA ✓
   legal knowledge.

4. Some plants can perform ___photosynthesis___ with very little light. ✓
   PYSENOTSHOTHSI

5. On a clear night, the stars and moon make the whole sky appear ___luminous___. ✓
   OSUMLNIU

6. The clever teacher was able to ___elucidate___ the chemistry concept, so most of the students were ✓
   ETIDAECLU
   successful with the experiment.

7. When the power went out, the family used candles to ___illuminate___ the room. ✓
   METLALUINI

Chapter 4:
Exercises

------------------------------ *Word Bank* ------------------------------

luminous   illuminate   elucidate   photosynthesis

luminary   lucid   photon

VIII. Write About It!

DIRECTIONS: In this chapter, you have learned words about light and its travels. Pick a favorite hobby or activity and write about how you would become a *luminary* in that hobby or activity.

_____

_____

_____

_____

_____

_____

_____

_____

_____

_____

Growing Your Vocabulary: Learning from Latin and Greek Roots

Projectile

Interject

Eject   Motive

Dejected

Remote

Immobile

Mobile

Remove

Motivate

Growing Your Vocabulary: Learning from Latin and Greek Roots

mob   ject

mot/mov

Chapter 5:
On the Move

This chapter is all about words that have to do with mobility and going from one place to another.

Roots to Learn:	**Words to Learn:**		**Prefixes:**
ject mot/mov mob	projectile eject interject dejected mobile	immobile remove remote motive motivate	e– inter– de–

noun

PROJECTILE comes from the Latin prefix *pro–*, meaning "forth " or "forward," and the verb **JACERE, JECTUS**, meaning "to throw." From this Latin verb, we get the root **JECT**. So, a **PROJECTILE** is an object that is thrown or propelled.

verb

By combining the prefix e– and the root *ject*, we get the word **EJECT**.

EJECT means "to throw out." *verb*

*The player was **ejected** from the game because the stick she used was too large.*

Do now

verb

I motivate myself in swimming with wanting to get better times.

My motivation for swimming is getting better times.

PREFIX ALARM!
The prefix e– means "out" or "away."
Example:
e– + *merge* = emerge—to come out or away from

INTERJECT means "to cut in" or "to break the flow." *Verb*

*Bud and Drew argued until Nancy **interjected** that the restaurant was closing.*

Did You Know?

Several sports have rules about interference, which happens when one player illegally comes between another player and some object or the goal. In baseball, blocking someone who is trying to run to a base is considered interference. In basketball, blocking a ball that is going down toward the basket is also a type of interference, called "goaltending."

PREFIX ALARM!

The prefix *inter–* means "between" or "among."
Example:
inter– + *section* = intersection—the point where two or more things cross or meet

*Gayle looks **dejected** because she thinks everyone forgot her birthday.*

DEJECTED means "downcast" or "sad." *adj.*

When you see or hear the word **DEJECTED**, think of its literal meaning: "thrown" or "cast down."

PREFIX ALARM!

The prefix *de–* means "down," "away," or "opposite."
Example:
de– + *value* = devalue—to make less important or special than in the past

The Latin word **MOBILIS** means "moving." From this word, we get the root **MOB**.

adj

MOBILE means "able to move."

Why are cell phones called **MOBILE** phones? You already know the answer, just by knowing what the word means!

I THINK WE'VE GOT JUST ABOUT EVERYTHING.

DIAPERS   TOYS

*Mom and I put together a **mobile** nursery for taking my baby brother to daycare.*

adj-

IMMOBILE means "not able to move."

One major difference between plants and animals is that plants cannot move from one place to another for food. Some plants, like sunflowers, can move to catch more sun, but they cannot move from their location. Therefore, plants are **IMMOBILE**.

WASHINGTON MIDDLE-SCHOOL
WE'RE GROWING!

*The new classrooms were moved by truck, but now they are set up and **immobile**.*

Chapter 5:
On the Move

The Latin word that means "to move" has two parts that are important to us: **MOVERE** and **MOTUS**. From these two parts we get the roots **MOV** and **MOT**.

To **REMOVE** means "to change *verb* position" or "to take away."

REMOTE means "moved away from" *adj* or "distant."

Now you know why the instrument that changes the channels on your TV is called a **REMOTE**.

Who is in charge of the remote at your house?

*The journalists set up a satellite connection on the **remote** mountain campsite.*

A **MOTIVE** is a person's reason for doing something or what moves someone to action—a reason. *noun*

To **MOTIVATE** is to urge into action.

You may have heard of a "**MOTIVATIONAL** speaker." He or she encourages people to take action, to make their lives better, happier, or more productive. Motivational speakers give people reasons and ways to improve.

Growing Your Vocabulary: Learning from Latin and Greek Roots

Exercises
Word Bank

projectile	interject	mobile	remove	motive
eject	dejected	immobile	remote	motivate

I. Define It! (Part 1)

DIRECTIONS: Write the letter of the word from the right column that matches the definition in the left column. The first one has been done for you.

1. to throw out **E**
2. able to move **H**
3. to take away **D**
4. moved away from; distant **F**
5. to interrupt **C**
6. unable to move **A**
7. downcast or sad **G**
8. that which moves someone; a driving cause **B**
9. to urge into action **J**
10. an object thrown forward **I**

A. immobile
B. motive
C. interject
D. remove
E. eject
F. remote
G. dejected
H. mobile
I. projectile
J. motivate

II. Select It!

DIRECTIONS: Using the root, write a word to complete each sentence.
The first one has been done for you.

1. A _____**mobile**_____ library brings books to some small communities once a week. (Root = MOB)
2. Brady likes to wear costumes, but he had to _____remove_____ his mask so he wouldn't scare his little sister. (Root = MOV)
3. The speaker asked members of the audience to _____interject_____ any comments or questions they might have, and she would answer them. (Root = JECT)
4. When Susie and Tom hiked into the Grand Canyon, they lost their map and ended up in a(n) _____remote_____ location far from any ranger stations. (Root = MOT)
5. Ellen's _____motive_____ for sticking to her diet is to lose 5 pounds. (Root = MOT)
6. The dog was _____dejected_____ when he brought his owner a ball, and she refused to play with him. (Root = JECT)
7. Jina took the wheels off her chair in order to make it _____immobile_____. (Root = MOB)
8. The toy became a(n) _____projectile_____ when Tim hurled it across the room. (Root = JECT)
9. Planning a family vacation in Paris will _____motivate_____ all of us to save money. (Root = MOT)
10. I was surprised to see the toaster _____eject_____ the bread before it was toasted. (Root = JECT)

········· *Word Bank* ·········

| projectile | interject | mobile | remove | motive |
| eject | dejected | immobile | remote | motivate |

III. Define It! (Part 2)

DIRECTIONS: Based on what you have learned in this chapter, define each of the following in your own words, and create a sentence using the word.

1. eject: _____
_____

2. interject: _____
_____

3. dejected: _____
_____

4. mobile: _____
_____

5. immobile: _____
_____

6. remove: _____
_____

7. remote: _____
_____

8. motive: _____
_____

9. projectile: _____
_____

10. motivate: _____
_____

IV. Personalize It!

DIRECTIONS: Using your understanding of the vocabulary words, respond to the following prompts. Use a separate piece of paper if necessary.

1. If you had to *remove* one item from your room, what would it be? Why?
_____

2. Some classes are taught by using a satellite that shows a teacher in a *remote* location. How would a class like this be different from your current classes? What would you like or dislike about learning this way? Explain.
_____

3. Describe a situation in which you were responsible for another person feeling *dejected*. What could you do differently in the future to prevent something like that happening again?
_____

4. Sometimes, people need *motives* for doing things. If you were trying to convince your classmates to study hard for a test, what would you tell them their *motive* should be?
_____

Growing Your Vocabulary: Learning from Latin and Greek Roots

················· *Word Bank* ·················

projectile	interject	mobile	remove	motive
eject	dejected	immobile	remote	motivate

V. Decode It!

DIRECTIONS: Use what you have learned about the roots *ject*, *mob*, *mov*, and *mot* and the prefixes in this chapter to answer the following questions:

1. You have learned that the prefix *in–* means "not." The prefix *in–* also means "in" or "into." Review the root *ject*. What do you think the word *inject* means? Provide an example of how you might use the word.

   _____

   _____

2. The suffix *–tion* is used to create a noun from a verb. It means the "act or instance of something." In this chapter, you learned the definition for the words *motive* and *motivate*. What do you think the word *motivation* means? Use it in a sentence.

   _____

   _____

3. Review the prefix *in–* and read the following sentence: The doctor injected the vaccine into the patient's arm. What does the word *injected* mean in this sentence?

   _____

   _____

4. Remember *pro–* in *projectile*? *Project* is a word with more than one meaning and pronunciation. What do you think are two of the different meanings?

   _____

   _____

Word Bank

projectile	interject	mobile	remove	motive
eject	dejected	immobile	remote	motivate

VI. Compare It!

DIRECTIONS: In this chapter, two of the words are antonyms of one another. *Immobile* means "not able to be moved," and *mobile* means "able to be moved." For each of the vocabulary words, find an antonym, or a phrase that can be used as an antonym, and then use it correctly in a sentence.

1. eject:

_____

2. interject:

_____

3. dejected:

_____

4. remove:

_____

5. remote:

_____

6. motive:

_____

7. mobile:

_____

8. projectile:

_____

9. immobile:

_____

10. motivate:

_____

·········· *Word Bank* ··········

projectile	interject	mobile	remove	motive
eject	dejected	immobile	remote	motivate

VII. Put It In Context!

DIRECTIONS: For each vocabulary word, write a detailed sentence that explains the meaning of the word through the context of the sentence. You may change the part of speech to fit your sentences.

1. eject:

_____

_____

2. interject:

_____

_____

3. dejected:

_____

_____

4. mobile:

_____

_____

5. immobile:

_____

_____

6. remove:

_____

_____

7. remote:

_____

_____

8. motive:

_____

_____

9. projectile:

_____

_____

10. motivation:

_____

_____

Chapter 5:
Exercises

VIII. Solve It!

DIRECTIONS: Use the clues and words from this chapter to complete the crossword puzzle. Some of the words may be a different part of speech.

Word Bank

- eject
- interject
- dejected
- mobile
- immobile
- remove
- remote
- motive
- projectile
- ~~motivate~~

(handwritten answers filled in crossword grid)

Clues:

ACROSS

1. A coach will often give speeches in order to _____ a team.
6. A person who feels _____ might spend a lot of time crying and sitting alone.
8. Airplane pilots must know how to _____ themselves safely from their seats.
9. One _____ for studying is getting good grades.
10. The bat became a _____ when it slipped out of the hitter's hands as she swung it.

DOWN

2. If you constantly _____ your opinion when other people are trying to have a conversation, you will be considered rude.
3. By erasing words from the chalkboard, you _____ them.
4. You must remain like this while getting stitches.
5. Cars, trains, airplanes, skateboards, and in-line skates can all help you be _____.
7. From the viewpoint of someone in the United States, Europe is a _____ location.

Unscramble the letters in the circles in the crossword puzzle to make a word that fits in the blank in the sentence below. The unscrambled word is not one of the vocabulary words from this lesson, but it is related to some of them.

I am a word that means something you get similar to a vaccination.

injection

Word Bank

projectile	interject	mobile	remove	motive
eject	dejected	immobile	remote	motivate

IX. Write About It!

DIRECTIONS: The word *reject* means "to refuse something." Imagine that you are the editor of a poetry magazine, and someone has submitted a poem to you for publication. Choose one of the following reasons for not accepting the poem:

- the topic was not interesting
- there was not enough content

Then, write the person a *rejection* letter that explains why the poem was *rejected*. Use the word *rejected*, as well as at least three other vocabulary words from this chapter, in your letter.

_____

_____

_____

_____

_____

_____

_____

_____

_____

_____

Review It!

DIRECTIONS: Read each question. Then, circle the letter next to the best answer.

1. The root in the word *progeny* means
   A. movement.
   B. birth.
   C. five.
   D. light.
   E. skin

2. What does the word *cardiovascular* mean?
   A. having to do with the heart and veins
   B. depending on light to make food
   C. the study of the skin
   D. measure
   E. occurring before birth

3. Read the sentence below:

   We knew that if we walked out of the room during Karen's speech, it would *mortify* her.

   Which word means the same as mortify?
   A. injure
   B. release
   C. kill
   D. embarrass
   E. please

4. The prefix *inter–* in the word *interject* means
   A. beneath.
   B. between.
   C. above.
   D. out of.
   E. into.

5. If you are feeling *dejected*, you are probably
   A. smiling.
   B. waving.
   C. winking.
   D. frowning.
   E. yawning.

6. If you do not have enough red blood cells, you may have
   A. acne.
   B. laryngitis.
   C. migraines.
   D. anemia.
   E. angina.

Review It!

7. Which of the following would be most likely to be *immobile*?
   A. a car
   B. a tree
   C. a shark
   D. a sled
   E. a missile

8. The root *lumin* in the word *illuminate* comes from the Latin word meaning
   A. birth.
   B. light.
   C. to throw.
   D. to survive.
   E. to move.

9. The prefix *im–* in the word *immobile* means
   A. into.
   B. between.
   C. forward.
   D. outside.
   E. not.

10. Read the sentence below:

    The magazines Stephanie reads do not seem to fit a particular *genre*.

    The italicized word means
    A. reason.
    B. light.
    C. gene.
    D. category.
    E. offspring.

11. Which word is the best antonym for *lucid*?
    A. typical
    B. sad
    C. alive
    D. unclear
    E. moveable

12. If something is *morbid*, it is
    A. sick or unhealthy.
    B. painful.
    C. flavorful.
    D. unreal.
    E. ancient.

13. If you are studying *dermatology*, you must be
    A. learning about the heart.
    B. learning about the skin.
    C. taking care of babies.
    D. seeing how plants use light.
    E. finding out why some people live longer.

14. What does the word *vivacious* mean?
    A. full of light
    B. able to die
    C. present at birth
    D. full of energy
    E. using light for food

15. Which is the best synonym for *motivate*?
    A. remove
    B. sadden
    C. encourage
    D. create
    E. anger

16. Read the sentence below:

    Carl had many *motives* for helping his neighbor clean her garage.

    The word *motives* means
    A. reasons.
    B. categories.
    C. thrown objects.
    D. children.
    E. dreams.

17. The suffix *–ous* in the word *luminous* means
    A. creating.
    B. one who.
    C. resembling.
    D. full of.
    E. the study of.

18. Which of these Latin roots means "birth," kind," or "type"?
    A. viv
    B. gen
    C. nat
    D. luc
    E. mort

Growing Your Vocabulary: Learning from Latin and Greek Roots

Review It!

19. The Greek root meaning "light" appears in which of the following words?
    A. photon
    B. cardiology
    C. epidermis
    D. anemia
    E. gene

20. The prefix *post-* means "after." The word *postnatal* means
    A. after motion.
    B. after death.
    C. after blood loss.
    D. after sunrise.
    E. after birth.

21. Which of the following could be *congenital*?
    A. a child from the same family
    B. a reason for acting
    C. the outside of the skin
    D. something thrown through the air
    E. a heart problem present at birth

22. The best synonym for the word *elucidate* is
    A. throw.
    B. study.
    C. move.
    D. clarify.
    E. die.

23. People's lives end, but the Greek gods were believed to be
    A. immortal.
    B. projectile.
    C. lucid.
    D. generic.
    E. immobile.

24. The best antonym for the word *remote* is
    A. mobile.
    B. nearby.
    C. cheerful.
    D. dark.
    E. unclear.

Gravitate

Aggravate

Grave

Appendix

Pendulum

Pendant

Pensive

Pending

Growing Your Vocabulary: Learning from Latin and Greek Roots

grav

pend

pens

Chapter 6:
Gravity Is Good for Everyone

Have you heard the story about Sir Isaac Newton and the apple? It is a popular tale about how Newton formed his theories about gravity. A few words in this chapter relate to gravity in some way.

Roots to Learn:	**Words to Learn:**	**Suffixes:**
grav pend/pens	grave pendant gravitate appendix aggravate pending pendulum pensive	–ant –ive

GRAVITY is the mysterious force by which all objects with mass attract other objects. The word **GRAVITY** comes from the Latin adjective, **GRAVIS**, which means "heavy." The root **GRAV** comes from **GRAVIS**.

GRAVE means "gloomy; causing heaviness of spirit" or "serious."

You might ask, "What is the relationship between 'grave' and 'gravity'?" Think of it like this: Gravity is a force that *pulls* things together. When someone is grave, he or she is being *pulled* down.

*Kelsey has a **grave** challenge ahead of her if she wants to win the election.*

Chapter 6:
Gravity Is Good for Everyone

In Chapter 1, you learned that the suffix *–ate* means "to cause to be" or "to make."

To **GRAVITATE** is to cause to move forward.

You **GRAVITATE** toward what you like or what you do well because that particular thing "pulls" you. A sport or hobby you like can attract you and you will gravitate toward it.

*Photographers **gravitate** toward the actor.*

The Latin verb **GRAVARE** means "to burden." The root **GRAV** comes from **GRAVARE**, as well as from **GRAVIS**.

*Smog **aggravates** Mary's cough.*

AGGRAVATE means "to make worse" or "to make more serious."

When something **AGGRAVATES** you, what do you do? To fix the cause of their aggravation, people try to make a serious situation less aggravating or less grave.

The Latin verb that means "to hang" has two parts that are important to us: **PENDERE** and **PENSUM**. From this verb, we get the roots **PEND** and **PENS**.

A **PENDULUM** is an object that hangs down and swings in a regular motion.

SUFFIX ALARM!
The suffix *–ant* is used to show that something is being acted upon.
Example: cool + *–ant* = coolant—something that is used to cool

A **PENDANT** usually refers to a piece of jewelry that hangs around the neck.

PENDANTS have been part of human history for thousands of years. At first, it is believed that people wore them for luck or to chase away evil spirits. Nowadays, though, pendants are mostly for decoration.

*A **pendant** in the shape of a heart hung on the gold chain.*

An **APPENDIX** is called by that name because it hangs on the book; it contains extra material.

Did You Know?
When you are using a textbook in class, you can find information you need by looking in the appendix. Most books have a glossary and index, but some books have even more information in an appendix.

*The new edition contains an **appendix** with updated notes.*

Chapter 6:
Gravity Is Good for Everyone

PENDING means "hanging" or "waiting."

New inventions frequently have the words *patent pending* on them. This means that a patent, which is issued by the government for every new product, is "waiting" to be released.

*The lawyer cannot comment on the case because it is still **pending**.*

*Doug was **pensive** as he worked on his third novel.*

From the idea of heaviness of mood we get the word **PENSIVE**.

PENSIVE means "deep in thought" or "worried."

Are you a pensive person? Do you think deeply about the world? Do you keep a journal or write poetry? Do you spend time staring at the clouds or a tree and thinking about serious problems? If so, you are growing up. Small children have difficulty being pensive because they are not ready to think deeply about the world, but you might have the maturity to thoughtfully consider complex issues. Of course, goofing off can be fun, too!

SUFFIX ALARM!
The suffix *–ive* means "performing a specific action."
Example:
disrupt + *–ive* = disruptive—causing a problem or interruption

Exercises
Word Bank

grave	aggravate	pendant	pending
gravitate	pendulum	appendix	pensive

I. Define It! (Part 1)

DIRECTIONS: Write the letter of the word from the right column that matches the definition in the left column. The first one has been done for you.

1. to make more serious **G**
2. waiting **B**
3. deep in thought or worried **D**
4. gloomy; causing heaviness of spirit **C**
5. a piece of jewelry that hangs around the neck **F**
6. to move toward **E**
7. an object that hangs down and swings in a regular motion **H**
8. something attached to a written work **A**

A. appendix
B. pending
C. grave
D. pensive
E. gravitate
F. pendant
G. aggravate
H. pendulum

II. Select It!

DIRECTIONS: Using the root, write a word to complete each sentence. The first one has been done for you.

1. The situation was becoming _**grave**_ for the baby panda after it had not eaten for three days. (Root = GRAV)
2. In the _Appendix_ of his science book, Oliver found diagrams of the tiny organisms he had read about. (Root = PEND)
3. The young kids _Gravitated_ toward the dance floor every time the DJ played hip-hop music. (Root = GRAV)
4. As the teacher walked around the room, she could tell that the students had not studied for the exam because of the _pensive_ looks on their faces. (Root = PENS)
5. On Tricia's wedding day, her grandmother presented her with an antique diamond _pendent_ that had been passed down through four generations. (Root = PEND)
6. Plans to build a new community playground were _pending_ final approval from the town council. (Root = PEND)
7. The tire hanging from the tree branch swung like a(n) _pendulum_ in the warm breeze of a June afternoon. (Root = PEND)
8. The itchy wool jacket tended to _aggravate_ the sunburn on Adrian's back. (Root = GRAV)

Exercises

grave	aggravate	pendant	pending
gravitate	pendulum	appendix	pensive

III. Define It! (Part 2)

DIRECTIONS: Based on what you have learned in this chapter, define each of the following in your own words, and create a sentence using the word.

1. grave: _Grave is when it is glommy or serious._

2. gravitate: _when you gravitate towards someone you move towards someone or something._

3. aggravate: _To aggravate is to make something more serious._

4. pendulum: _I something that swings back and fourth_

5. pendant: _a necklace or something that hangs from your neck._

6. appendix: _the back of a book_

7. pending: _waiting_

8. pensive: _deep in thought_

IV. Personalize It!

DIRECTIONS: Using your understanding of the vocabulary words, respond to the following prompts. Use a separate piece of paper if necessary.

1. We have all been *aggravated* by something or someone. Describe your biggest pet peeve, and explain why it *aggravates* you.

   My biggest pet peeve is when

2. Describe a *grave* situation, and explain why it was so depressing or sad.

   When your dog dies.

3. When was the last time you saw someone looking *pensive*? What do you think might have been on the person's mind?

   they were nervous for someone

4. If you wanted to create an *appendix* to your school handbook, what information would it include and why?

   definitions of words

········· *Word Bank* ·········

| grave | aggravate | pendant | pending |
| gravitate | pendulum | appendix | pensive |

V. Decode It!

DIRECTIONS: Use what you have learned about the roots *grav*, *pend*, and *pens* and the suffixes in this chapter to answer the following questions:

1. Review the root *grav* and the suffixes *–tion* and *–al*. They are used to create the word *gravitational*. The United States has a well-developed space program. Astronauts often use the term *gravitational pull* to describe the attraction between large objects like earth and the sun. What effect does the sun's *gravitational* pull have on Earth?

   _____

   _____

   _____

2. One meaning of the prefix *a–* is "on." What do you think *append* means? Use what you know about the root *pend* to use *append* in a sentence.

   _____

   _____

   _____

3. Add the suffix *–tion* to a word from this chapter to mean "the act of making something worse." Then use the word in a sentence.

   _____

   _____

   _____

4. When a doctor diagnoses *appendicitis*, or inflammation of the appendix, she may recommend an *appendectomy*. An *appendectomy* is surgery to remove the appendix. What do you think the suffixes *–itis* and *–ectomy* mean?

   _____

   _____

   _____

·········· *Word Bank* ··········

grave	aggravate	pendant	pending
gravitate	pendulum	appendix	pensive

VI. Unscramble It!

DIRECTIONS: The vocabulary words from the chapter have been scrambled. Using the synonym, figure out which vocabulary word belongs in the blank. Then, unscramble the letters to write the word correctly.

1. supplementary material *Appendix*
   AXDPEPNI

2. necklace *pendent*
   DAPETNN

3. move toward *gravitate*
   AGAETRVIT

4. thoughtful *pensive*
   NEPVSIE

5. serious *grave* .
   RGVEA

6. bother *aggravate*
   VAGARGETA

7. awaiting *pending*
   NIPNEDG

8. something that swings in a regular motion *pendulum*
   LPUDNEMU

.... *Word Bank* ....

grave	aggravate	pendant	pending
gravitate	pendulum	appendix	pensive

VII. Match It!

DIRECTIONS: Read each of the following sentences. The vocabulary word has been left out of the sentence. Match the vocabulary word to the sentence in which it would fit.

1. The students raised money for the tornado-stricken town because they wanted to help the _____**grave**_____ situation the people were in.
2. When Beau read a story in his literature book, he checked the ___*appendix*___ to find the definitions of unknown words.
3. My little sister can ___*aggravate*___ me, but I try not to let her constant questions bother me too much.
4. Aaron got an "A" ___*pendant*___ that hangs from his keychain.
5. After setting the world record for playing on a swing for three days in a row, Kim became known as the "human ___*pendulum*___."
6. The best friends tended to ___*gravitate*___ toward one another in class and constantly got in trouble for talking.
7. The ___*pensive*___ little boy sat quietly and tried to solve his math problems.
8. ___*pending*___ a weather report, the ski trip may or may not be cancelled.

VIII. Analogies!

DIRECTIONS: For each of the vocabulary words in the chapter, complete the analogy.

1. *Big* is to *large* as *disturb* is to _____.
2. *Purple* is to *violet* as _____ is to *thoughtful*.
3. _____ is to *car accident* as *festive* is to *awards assembly*.
4. _____ is to *avoid* as *fat* is to *thin*.
5. *Epilogue* is to *play* as _____ is to *reference book*.
6. *Award* is to *certificate* as *medal* is to _____.
7. *Football* is to *projectile* as *trapeze* is to _____.
8. *Finished* is to _____ as *summer* is to *winter*.

Alleviate

Levity

Levitate

Lever

Elevate

Relieve

Altitude

Exalt

Growing Your Vocabulary: Learning from Latin and Greek Roots

lev

alt

Chapter 7:
Flight—Keep It Light

Have you ever wondered how magicians are able to make people or things float above the ground? This chapter is about words that you can use to describe height, magic tricks, and helping others, but it is not about gravity or light.

Roots to Learn:	**Words to Learn:**	**Suffixes:**
lev alt	levity lever elevate relieve alleviate altitude levitate exalt	–y

The Latin adjective **LEVIS** means "lightweight," and the related verb **LEVARE**, **LEVATUM** means "to lift up."

LEVITY means "lightness of mood" or "humor." You might use **LEVITY** when the mood is getting too heavy.

Did You Know?

The word *happy* uses the suffix –y. The word *happy* was formed from the Middle English word for "luck." When the suffix –y was added, the meaning changed to "favored by luck." You probably thought that the word *happy* meant only "to be in good spirits."

*Barry thought the gloomy meeting could use a little **levity**.*

SUFFIX ALARM!
The suffix –y means "having the quality of" or "full of."
Examples:
chill + –y = chilly—having the quality of coldness
brain + –y = brainy—full of brains (very smart)

To **ELEVATE** is to lift up.

*My appearance on the local news **elevated** my popularity in town.*

> # Did You Know?
> The first passenger elevator was used in New York City in 1857. However, lifting a room up that is filled with people had happened much earlier. In ancient Egypt and Greece, animals pulled elevators to the tops of buildings.

DON'T FORGET THE CAN-OPENERS!

*Emergency supplies were rushed to the village to **alleviate** the hunger crisis.*

ALLEVIATE means "to make a pain or burden lighter."

A doctor can prescribe medication to **ALLEVIATE** the symptoms of a disease, and a friend can do the same for feelings of loneliness.

To **LEVITATE** means "to float above."

Have you ever seen a magician **LEVITATE** a person or an object? It looks real, but. hopefully, you know it is impossible. If there were no gravity (Remember this word from Chapter 6?), everything would levitate!

*The leaf blew upward and **levitated** for a moment above the tree.*

A **LEVER** is something that lifts.

LEVERS are very common, much more than you probably realize. A seesaw is an example of a lever; so is a diving board, a can opener, and a pair of pliers. Scissors are an example of two levers working at the same time. Handbrakes on a bike act as levers, too.

*A special **lever** lifted the heavy doors of the castle.*

To **RELIEVE** means "to give aid or help" or "to set free."

One way to **RELIEVE** stress is through exercise.

Pay attention to how all these words are related. *Alleviate, relieve, lever,* and *levitate* all have to do with making something rise up.

*The officer had been on her shift for more than twenty-four hours before someone came to **relieve** her.*

Growing Your Vocabulary: Learning from Latin and Greek Roots

Chapter 7:
Flight—Keep it Light

The Latin adjective **ALTUS** means "high." From its root **ALT**, we get the following words:

ALTITUDE refers to a distance of height.

9500...

*The skydivers jumped from an **altitude** of 9500 feet.*

Did You Know?

The higher you are in altitude, the less oxygen is in the air. Mountain climbers frequently experience what is called "altitude sickness" if they climb above 12,000 feet. That's why many of them use bottled oxygen—to help them breathe.

THE HILLS AND THE TREES SMELL FAR BETTER THAN CHEESE.

*The poet **exalted** nature and the beauty of the natural world in her writing.*

To **EXALT** means "to look up to" or "to think very highly of."

EXALT might be a difficult vocabulary word because, most of the time, you think of ex– as meaning "not" or "without," as an ex-friend. In this case, though, ex– means "from." The word exalt, then, means "from height." That is how something is exalted—you think of it as it is raised up high.

Growing Your Vocabulary: Learning from Latin and Greek Roots

Exercises

Word Bank

levity	alleviate	lever	altitude
elevate	levitate	relieve	exalt

I. Define It! (Part 1)

DIRECTIONS: Write the letter of the word from the right column that matches the definition in the left column. The first one has been done for you.

1. to lift up **D**

2. lightness of mood; humor ___

3. to make a burden or pain lighter ___

4. to float above ___

5. to raise on high; to glorify ___

6. height ___

7. to give help or to set free ___

8. something that lifts ___

A. exalt

B. relieve

C. levitate

D. elevate

E. levity

F. alleviate

G. lever

H. altitude

II. Finish It!

DIRECTIONS: Using the root, write a word to complete each sentence.
The first one has been done for you.

1. When they finally reached the top of the mountain, the climbers were at a higher _____**altitude**_____ than the clouds. (Root = ALT)

2. The mechanic had to use a special _____ in order to lift the car off the garage floor. (Root = LEV)

3. The magician began his show by _____ his assistant above the table. (Root = LEV)

4. Mary was _____ when her Spanish teacher announced that the test had been rescheduled, because she had forgotten to study. (Root = LEV)

5. Garry's _____ made all his guests feel cheerful and lighthearted. (Root = LEV)

6. After a long day at work, the salesclerk had to _____ his legs to reduce the swelling in his knees. (Root = LEV)

7. In India, the cow is a(n) _____ animal; people there have great respect for cows. (Root = ALT)

8. The camp counselor allowed Deja to call her parents to _____ her terrible homesickness. (Root = LEV)

··· *Word Bank* ···

levity	alleviate	lever	altitude
elevate	levitate	relieve	exalt

III. Define It! (Part 2)

DIRECTIONS: Based on what you have learned in this chapter, define each of the following in your own words, and create a sentence using the word.

1. levity: _____

_____

2. elevate: _____

_____

3. alleviate: _____

_____

4. levitate: _____

_____

5. lever: _____

_____

6. relieve: _____

_____

7. altitude: _____

_____

8. exalt: _____

_____

····················· *Word Bank* ·····················

| levity | alleviate | lever | altitude |
| elevate | levitate | relieve | exalt |

IV. Compare It!

DIRECTIONS: For each of the vocabulary words in the chapter, find an antonym for the word and then use it correctly in a sentence.

1. levity:

_____

_____

2. alleviate:

_____

_____

3. relieve:

_____

_____

4. exalt:

_____

_____

5. levitate:

_____

_____

6. altitude:

_____

_____

7. elevate:

_____

_____

········· *Word Bank* ·········

levity	alleviate	lever	altitude
elevate	levitate	relieve	exalt

V. Acrostic Challenge!

DIRECTIONS: Fill in the blank spaces below with the words that are defined by the clues. Then, use the letters in the circles to solve for the missing word.

1. to glorify __ __ __ Ⓞ __

2. to lift up Ⓞ __ __ __ __ __ __

3. humor __ __ Ⓞ __ __ __

4. to make someone's burden lighter __ __ __ Ⓞ __ __ __ __ __

5. a tool used to move something __ __ __ Ⓞ __

6. height Ⓞ __ __ __ __ __ __ __

7. helping someone in need __ __ __ __ __ __ __ Ⓖ

8. to float above __ Ⓞ __ __ __ __ __

What is something you use to get an advantage over someone else?

__ __ __ __ __ __ __

VI. Decode It!

DIRECTIONS: Use words from the word bank to answer the following questions:

1. In a male chorus, an *alto* singer is a man who has a higher voice than other men. The term *contralto* includes the prefix *contra–*, which means "against" or "opposite." This term is usually reserved for women with what kind of voice?

    _____

2. The suffix *–able* means "possible to do." What do you think *relievable* means?

    _____

3. The suffix *–meter* describes a measure or a tool for measuring. What do you think an *altimeter* is?

    _____

Growing Your Vocabulary: Learning from Latin and Greek Roots

VII. Solve It!

Directions: Use the clues and words from this chapter to complete the crossword puzzle. Some of the words may be a different part of speech.

Word Bank

- levitate
- lever
- relieve
- altitude
- levity
- elevate
- alleviate
- exalt

Clues:

ACROSS

2. The medicine I took was almost useless; it just didn't _____ my allergies.

4. You need to have enough of this if you are going to jump out of an airplane.

7. A person should not use this at a somber event.

8. In the movie, the character just floats up, like magic.

DOWN

1. Jeremiah thought he had failed the math test, but he was _____ when he got a B on it.

3. You can write a song of praise to do this to someone.

5. A toilet bowl handle is an example of this.

6. If you make someone happy, you do this to her mood.

Unscramble the letters in the circles in the crossword puzzle to make a word that answers the riddle below. The unscrambled word is not one of the vocabulary words from this lesson, but it is related to some of them.

I can take you to the top of a tall building or to the basement. __ __ __ __ __ __ **O** __

··· Word Bank ·······································

| levity | alleviate | lever | altitude |
| elevate | levitate | relieve | exalt |

VIII. Write About It!

DIRECTIONS: In this chapter, you have learned words about flight and "keeping it light." Write a paragraph describing a situation in which it would be appropriate to show *levity*.

_____

_____

_____

_____

_____

_____

_____

_____

_____

_____

Capture

Captivate

Captive

Accept

Recipient

Participate

Intercept

Anticipate

Except

Growing Your Vocabulary: Learning from Latin and Greek Roots

capt

cip

cept

Chapter 8:
Give and Take

Have you ever been captivated by a good book or movie? This chapter is all about words that deal with capture and receipt.

Roots to Learn:
capt   cip cept

Words to Learn:	
capture	intercept
captive	anticipate
captivate	recipient
accept	participate
except	

The Latin verb **CAPERE**, **CAPTUS** means "to take." The roots **CAPT**, **CEPT**, and **CIP** are all roots from this word. We get many words from the roots **CAPT**, **CEPT**, and **CIP**.

To **CAPTURE** means "to take."

A **CAPTIVE** is someone who has been taken.

To **CAPTIVATE** is to seize someone's attention or to fascinate.

Can you see how these words and ideas are similar? Don't get confused, but a captive can be taken into captivity by a captor only after he or she has been captured.

Rap sensation Little Julius has ***captured*** *the hearts of fans nationwide.*

ACCEPT means "to allow" or "to take in."

> **Did You Know?**
> *Accept* and *except* are *homophones*—words that sound the same but have different meanings. Can you think of other homophones? List some. Here's an example: *break* and *brake*.

*Jo could not **accept** the fact that her master was gone.*

*Everyone is eating an apple **except** Shrila—she's not enjoying her banana.*

EXCEPT is most often used to mean "not included," "but," "left out," "besides," or "unless."

Now that you know the difference between **ACCEPT** and **EXCEPT**, which word would go in the following sentences?

Marie would have gone, _____ she lost her ticket.

Marie could not _____ losing her ticket.

To **INTERCEPT** something is to catch or stop it between its beginning and end.

You don't have to **INTERCEPT** something with your hands, however. You could easily intercept a telephone call. One way to remember the word is that it is *interrupting* the flow of something.

*Kevin **intercepted** the football with 30 seconds to go in the game.*

ANTICIPATE means "to expect."

In order for Kevin to intercept the football in the previous cartoon, he must have **ANTICIPATED** where it would be so he could catch it!

*No one **anticipated** the amount of snow we got last March.*

*Geena was glad she **participated** in the science fair because she won a prize.*

PARTICIPATE means "to take part in."

Modern inventions let you **PARTICIPATE** in things without even being in the room. What new inventions do you think there will be in the next 10 years that allow you to take in numerous events at once?

A **RECIPIENT** is someone who gets something.

Have you ever been the **RECIPIENT** of an award? We hope that you'll learn vocabulary well enough to be the recipient of an English prize one day.

*For his tireless efforts to maintain peace between the countries, he was this year's Nobel Prize **recipient**.*

Growing Your Vocabulary: Learning from Latin and Greek Roots

Exercises
Word Bank

capture	captivate	except	anticipate	participate
captive	accept	intercept	recipient	

I. Define It! (Part 1)

DIRECTIONS: Write the letter of the word from the right column that matches the definition in the left column. The first one has been done for you.

1. to seize someone's attention; to fascinate __I__   A. capture
2. to take something in the middle of its journey ___   B. intercept
3. not including ___   C. except
4. to allow; to take in ___   D. recipient
5. to take part ___   E. participate
6. to expect ___   F. accept
7. someone who is taken ___   G. captive
8. to take ___   H. anticipate
9. someone who gets something ___   I. captivate

II. Finish It!

DIRECTIONS: Using the root, write a word to complete each sentence.
The first one has been done for you.

1. ____**Captivated**____ by the drama on the television news program, the babysitter did not notice the ringing doorbell. (Root = CAPT)

2. The goal of the game is to _____ the flag from the other team and return it to home base. (Root = CAPT)

3. Everyone was allowed to watch the game for free _____ for the fans who forgot to wear the team colors. (Root = CEPT)

4. We _____ that it would rain during the field trip because the weather reporter predicted a 90% chance of precipitation. (Root = CIP)

5. The crew took the pirates _____ once they took over the pirate ship. (Root = CAPT)

6. The secret agent wrote his message in code in case the enemy _____ it. (Root = CEPT)

7. The principal graciously _____ the invitation to have lunch with the sixth grade class. (Root = CEPT)

8. After rescuing the family from the rushing water, the firefighter was the _____ of the key to the city. (Root = CIP)

9. Bethany was chosen to _____ in the youth leadership conference because she was a positive role model in the school. (Root = CIP)

······· *Word Bank* ·······

capture	captivate	except	anticipate	participate
captive	accept	intercept	recipient	

III. Define It! (Part 2)

DIRECTIONS: Based on what you have learned in this chapter, define each of the following in your own words, and create a sentence using the word.

1. capture: _____

_____

2. captive: _____

_____

3. accept: _____

_____

4. except: _____

_____

5. intercept: _____

_____

6. anticipate: _____

_____

7. participate: _____

_____

8. recipient: _____

_____

9. captivate: _____

_____

IV. Personalize It!

DIRECTIONS: Using your understanding of the vocabulary words, respond to the following prompts. Use a separate piece of paper if necessary.

1. What is something that *captivates* you?

_____

2. Have you noticed that in middle school sometimes people your age have a difficult time *accepting* people they do not know? Why do you think it is hard for teenagers to *accept* people who are not exactly like them?

_____

3. Describe an event that you *anticipated* for a long time before it happened.

_____

4. Describe the activities in which you *participate*.

_____

-- Word Bank --

| capture | captivate | except | anticipate | participate |
| captive | accept | intercept | recipient | |

V. Compare It! (Synonyms)

DIRECTIONS: The vocabulary words in this chapter have synonyms that will help you learn the meaning of the word. Match the vocabulary word with a word or phrase that means something similar to it.

1. admit **F**
2. earner ___
3. block or obstruct ___
4. take prisoner ___
5. hostage ___
6. draw in ___
7. expect ___
8. besides ___
9. join in ___

A. capture
B. intercept
C. except
D. recipient
E. participate
F. accept
G. captive
H. anticipate
I. captivate

VI. Compare It! (Antonyms)

DIRECTIONS: The vocabulary words in this chapter have antonyms that will help you remember the meaning of the word. Match the vocabulary word with its antonym.

1. decline **E**
2. set free ___
3. donor ___
4. be surprised ___
5. push away ___
6. captor ___
7. included ___
8. observe ___
9. let pass ___

A. capture
B. except
C. recipient
D. participate
E. accept
F. captive
G. anticipate
H. captivate
I. intercept

········· *Word Bank* ·········

capture	captivate	except	anticipate	participate
captive	accept	intercept	recipient	

VII. Put It In Context!

DIRECTIONS: Complete the sentence in a way that shows you understand what the vocabulary word in italics means.

1. To avoid *capture*, the mouse…

_____

2. The dogs were held *captive*…

_____

3. The storyteller was able to *captivate* the audience by…

_____

4. The club would *accept* anyone who…

_____

5. The whole family traveled to Canada *except* Jamal, who…

_____

6. I tried to *intercept*…

_____

7. Most students *anticipate*…

_____

8. We decided to *participate* in…

_____

9. The *recipient* of a $500 bonus was…

_____

.... *Word Bank* ....

capture	captivate	except	anticipate	participate
captive	accept	intercept	recipient	

VIII. Write About It!

DIRECTIONS: In this chapter, you have learned words that have to do with taking and receiving. Choose a main character from a book or a story you have read recently. Decide on an award that you think the character should receive. For example, you might give a character a "Bravery Award" because of how he or she stood up to peer pressure. Describe the award you would give the character, and be sure to explain why the *recipient* has earned it. You may even want to write a short *acceptance* speech that the character might give.

_____

_____

_____

_____

_____

_____

_____

_____

_____

_____

Subterranean

Inter

Tenant

Attrition

Continent

Tenure

Trite

Tenement

Growing Your Vocabulary: Learning from Latin and Greek Roots

ter

ten/tin

trit

Chapter 9:

Planet Earth, Our Home

For humans, Earth is the source of all the materials we need to survive, from wood for shelter to grain for food. In this chapter, you will learn words that are related to our world.

Roots to Learn:

ter   trit

ten/tin

Words to Learn:

inter   tenure
subterranean   continent
tenant   trite
tenement   attrition

Prefixes:

sub—

con—

The Latin noun **TERRA** means "earth." The root **TER** comes from this word.

To **INTER** is to bury.

SUBTERRANEAN means "underground."

*A day after the king was **interred**, the new queen took the throne.*

Did You Know?

What is the most common subterranean animal? Do you think the answer is "worms"? There are over 2,700 kinds of earthworms. Insects? There are more than 1,000,000 kinds of insects, and most of them are subterranean for part of their life, so if you answered "bugs," congratulations!

PREFIX ALARM!
The prefix *sub*– means "under" or "beneath."
Example:
sub– + *standard* = substandard—of a quality that is below the expected or normal

Growing Your Vocabulary: Learning from Latin and Greek Roots

Another word that you probably use often when you are talking about the earth is the word **CONTINENT**. You know that a **CONTINENT** is one of the seven large landmasses on the planet. When continents collide, they create earthquakes, mountains, and volcanoes. Let's learn the origins of this important word and some words related to it.

*Lisa was a **tenant** in the tenement until they tore it down.*

Continent comes from the Latin verb meaning "to hold": **TENERE, TENTUM**. This word gives us the root **TEN**, to form words such as:

A **TENANT** is someone who lives on land or in a house owned by someone else.

A **TENEMENT** is a large, run-down apartment building. At one time, it simply referred to any apartment building, but many landlords (who owned the land) did not keep up the apartments. **TENEMENT** now describes a large, decaying building with lots of problems.

....

TENURE is the period of time that a person holds a job.

Sometimes, teachers have to stay employed for a few years in order to earn **TENURE**. Ask some teachers in your school about tenure.

*During her **tenure** in office, she made many improvements across half the state.*

The root **TIN** also comes from the word **TENERE**, **TENTUM**. So, we finally get back to the word *continent*.

Continent literally means "that which is held together." A continent is a huge mass of land that stays in a solid piece, even as it drifts along on the molten rock beneath the earth's surface.

PREFIX ALARM!
The prefix *con*– means "together" or "jointly."
Example: con– + *current* = concurrent—occurring at the same time, together

*The **continent** of North America is between the Atlantic and Pacific oceans.*

*The lyrics on the second album are much better than the **trite** songs of the artist's early work.*

The Latin verb that means "to rub" or "to wear away" is **TERERE**, **TRITUS**. From this word, we get the root **TRIT**.

TRITE means "unoriginal" or "clichéd." Something that is **TRITE** is worn out by overuse. Good writers avoid trite words and phrases because they want their writing to be strong and more original.

ATTRITION is a gradual loss, a wearing away, or a weakening.

Many wars are called "battles of **ATTRITION**" because the better-supplied army usually wins due to the weaker army wearing down, both in material and in its desire to win.

*After the popular coach quit, we had an **attrition** problem because only two players remained.*

Growing Your Vocabulary: Learning from Latin and Greek Roots

Exercises
Word Bank

subterranean	tenant	tenure	trite
inter	tenement	continent	attrition

I. Define It! (Part I)

DIRECTIONS: Write the letter of the word from the right column that matches the definition in the left column. The first one has been done for you.

1. underground **H**
2. the length of time you do a certain job or hold a position ___
3. unoriginal; clichéd ___
4. a large, run-down apartment complex ___
5. a person who lives in an apartment or home but does not own it ___
6. to bury ___
7. gradual loss or weakening ___
8. one of seven main landmasses on Earth ___

A. continent

B. tenant

C. tenure

D. tenement

E. trite

F. attrition

G. inter

H. subterranean

II. Select It!

DIRECTIONS: Using the root, write a word to complete each sentence.
The first one has been done for you.

1. People complained that the dilapidated ____**tenement**____ had no hot water or heat, but the landlord did not fix the problems. (Root = TEN)

2. Many schools and some businesses give employees special benefits when they have _____, or when they've had their jobs for a long time. (Root = TEN)

3. When writing assignments for a class, students should be careful to avoid _____ language that does not sound creative or original. (Root = TRIT)

4. Gophers dig a series of complex _____ tunnels that include feeding and nesting areas. (Root = TER)

5. The _____ of the apartment upstairs practices piano every night. (Root = TEN)

6. In Egypt, pyramids were built above the tombs where the pharaohs were _____. (Root = TER)

7. After wearing a cast for six weeks, Tom had to go the physical therapist to reverse the _____ of the muscle strength in his arm. (Root = TRIT)

8. Africa, Asia, and North America are all _____. (Root = TIN)

subterranean	tenant	tenure	trite
inter	tenement	continent	attrition

III. Define It! (Part 2)

DIRECTIONS: Based on what you have learned in this chapter, define each of the following in your own words, and create a sentence using the word.

1. subterranean: _____

   _____

2. inter: _____

   _____

3. tenure: _____

   _____

4. continent: _____

   _____

5. tenement: _____

   _____

6. tenant: _____

   _____

7. trite: _____

   _____

8. attrition: _____

   _____

IV. Personalize It!

DIRECTIONS: Using your understanding of the vocabulary words, respond to the following prompts. Use a separate piece of paper if necessary.

1. Describe a *tenement*. Have you ever seen a *tenement* in the movies or read about one in a book? What do you think it was like to live in one 100 years ago?

   _____

   _____

2. List several *trite* phrases that you have heard before.

   _____

   _____

3. *Attrition* is the gradual weakening or loss of something. How could a club or organization suffer from a high rate of *attrition*?

   _____

   _____

4. If you had to live in a *subterranean* area, what would your home look like?

   _____

   _____

Word Bank

subterranean	tenant	tenure	trite
inter	tenement	continent	attrition

V. Decode It!

DIRECTIONS: Use what you have learned about the roots *ter*, *tin/ten*, and *trit* and the prefixes and suffixes in this chapter to answer the following questions:

1. Review the prefix *dis–*. What do you think it means to *disinter* something?

   _____

   _____

2. The prefix *extra–* means "beyond." The suffix *–ial* means "relating to." What is a word that might mean "something that occurs beyond or outside of the earth"?

   _____

   _____

3. Your teacher might tell you to avoid using *trite* phrases and to focus on being original. What do you think the root word *tritus* has to do with the meaning of *trite*?

   _____

   _____

4. Much of United States history is centered on exploring, gaining, navigating, and protecting land. What historical word or words formed from the root word *terra* relate to our need for land?

   _____

   _____

Growing Your Vocabulary: Learning from Latin and Greek Roots

---- *Word Bank* ----

subterranean	tenant	tenure	trite
inter	tenement	continent	attrition

VI. Unscramble It!

DIRECTIONS: The vocabulary words from the chapter have been scrambled. Using the sentence, figure out which word belongs in the blank. Then, unscramble the letters to write the word correctly.

1. People don't generally like to live in a(n) _____ because it is not well maintained.
   MENTEENT

2. My teacher did not like the phrase "take the bull by the horns" because it was _____.
   RTEIT

3. Ancient Egyptians _____ their rulers in elaborate tombs.
   ETRINRDE

4. Ants are considered _____ insects.
   TENAEANURBSR

5. Russia is the largest country on the Asian _____.
   TICNENTON

6. The teacher had been in the school so long that he had _____.
   TRUENE

7. The engineers calculated the amount of _____ of the bridge's support system and determined it was still very strong.
   TIRTAOITN

8. The landlord put up a notice to remind the _____ that garbage from the apartments was collected on Tuesdays and Fridays.
   NSTEANT

·· *Word Bank* ··

subterranean   tenant   tenure   trite
inter   tenement   continent   attrition

VII. Put It In Context!

DIRECTIONS: For each vocabulary word, write a detailed sentence that explains the meaning of the word through the context of the sentence. You may change the part of speech to fit your sentences.

1. The *subterranean* cavern was useful to the hikers…

   _____

2. The family could not *inter* the soldier until…

   _____

3. The school board granted the teacher *tenure* because…

   _____

4. The most interesting *continent* is _____ because…

   _____

5. If a *tenant* damages the apartment,…

   _____

6. While living in a *tenement*, Michael learned…

   _____

7. An example of a *trite* expression is…

   _____

8. People will experience an *attrition* of knowledge if…

   _____

VIII. Solve It!

DIRECTIONS: Use the clues and words from this chapter to complete the crossword puzzle. Some of the words may be a different part of speech.

Word Bank

subterranean

inter

continent

tenure

tenant

tenement

trite

attrition

Clues:

ACROSS

1. South America, Australia, and Asia are examples of this.

5. Animals that live in _____ dens might live their entire lives without ever seeing the sun.

6. When you describe a cliché, you might use this word.

7. A graveyard is where people _____ the dead.

8. The football team lost nine players due to injuries, leaving a weakened offense.

DOWN

2. Apartments in the huge _____ are cheap, but the building is overcrowded and poorly maintained.

3. A teacher who has been at a job a long time may have this.

4. Someone who lives on someone else's land or in someone else's home is one of these.

Unscramble the letters in the circles in the crossword puzzle to make a word that fits in the blanks in the sentence below. The unscrambled word is not one of the vocabulary words from this lesson, but it is related to some of them.

After putting in some dirt, rocks, plants, and water, I put a frog and a lizard

in the big ___ ___ ___ ___ ___ ___ ___ ___ ___ I keep in my room.

Growing Your Vocabulary: Learning from Latin and Greek Roots

Word Bank

subterranean	tenant	tenure	trite
inter	tenement	continent	attrition

IX. Write About It!

DIRECTIONS: In this chapter, you have learned words that have to do with the earth. Pretend that you are hired to write articles for an encyclopedia. Write a short encyclopedia entry that explains one of the following: how the earth's *continents* have moved over time, a short history of *tenements* in the United States, or a type of *subterranean* animal or insect.

_____

_____

_____

_____

_____

_____

_____

_____

_____

Homo Sapiens

Homicide

Misanthrope

Anthropology

Android

Philanthropy

Growing Your Vocabulary: Learning from Latin and Greek Roots

andro

anthropo

hom

Chapter 10:
Human Beings—
Bodies and Minds

The Greek philosopher Plato called man "a being in search of meaning." People spend a lot of time making sense of our role in the universe. We search our past, our actions, and our minds to learn about our nature and our purpose. The words in this chapter are about what makes us who we are.

Roots to Learn:	**Words to Learn:**	**Prefix:**	**Suffix:**
hom andro anthropo	Homo sapiens misanthrope homicide philanthropy anthropology android	mis–	–cide

The Latin noun **HOMO, HOMINIS** means "human" or "man." The root from this noun is **HOM**.

The Latin **HOMO SAPIENS** is the scientific name for human beings; it literally means "wise man."

The Latin word *homo–* refers to humans, but the Greek prefix *homo–* means "same." Words that contain the prefix *homo* include *homonym*, *homogenize*, and *homophone*.

A **HOMICIDE** is the murder of a human being.

*The earliest fossils of **Homo sapiens** have been found in Ethiopia.*

SUFFIX ALARM!
The suffix *–cide* comes from the Latin word *caedere*, meaning "to cut" or "to kill."
Examples: insect + i + –cide = insecticide—a poison that kills insects
pest + i + –cide = pesticide—a poison that kills pests

Growing Your Vocabulary: Learning from Latin and Greek Roots

Chapter 10:
Human Beings—
Bodies and Minds

The Greek noun **ANTHROPOS** means "man." From it, we get the root **ANTHROPO**, which is used to form words like the following:

> **ANTHROPOLOGY** is the study of human beings and their culture.

> If you were an **ANTHROPOLOGIST** from the future who was studying today's culture what one or two items would best show how society works?

*The first **anthropology** studies in America examined the culture of Native Americans.*

PREFIX ALARM!
The prefix *mis–* means "bad" or "wrong."
Example: mis– + lead = mislead—to lead someone the wrong way

COUNCIL MEETING

I DON'T KNOW WHY I LIVE IN A TOWN FILLED WITH SO MANY IMBECILES!

*That lady was labeled a **misanthrope** because she criticized her fellow citizens at town council meetings.*

A **MISANTHROPE** is someone who hates people.

Some famous **MISANTHROPES** in literature:
- Mr. Hyde
- Lex Luther
- The Joker
- Frankenstein's Monster
- Lord Voldemort
- Ebenezer Scrooge

PHILANTHROPY is the act of charitable giving.

Throughout the U.S.A., the average philanthropic contribution is $1,620, which totals almost $3,000,000,000 every year. Most of this money is given to educational and religious causes.

COLLEGE MONEY

COLLEGE MONEY

*The **philanthropist's** charitable contributions included providing scholarships to students to make their dreams come true.*

Growing Your Vocabulary: Learning from Latin and Greek Roots

Another Greek word for "man" is **ANDROS**. One word we get from the root **ANDRO** is:

An **ANDROID** is a machine or robot that resembles a human being.

If you were designing an **ANDROID**, what improvements would you want it to have over the way human beings function? For example, would it have 3 arms so it could work harder?

*This **android's** battery ran down before it could finish cleaning the room.*

Chapter 10:
Exercises

Exercises
Word Bank

Homo sapiens	anthropology	philanthropy
homicide	misanthrope	android

I. Define It! (Part 1)

DIRECTIONS: Write the letter of the word from the right column that matches the definition in the left column. The first one has been done for you.

1. charitable giving **F**

2. an artificial being that has some human qualities ___

3. the scientific name for human beings; it literally means "wise man." ___

4. the study of human beings and their culture ___

5. the murder of a human ___

6. someone who hates people ___

A. homicide

B. Homo sapiens

C. anthropology

D. misanthrope

E. android

F. philanthropy

II. Finish It!

DIRECTIONS: Using the root, write a word to complete each sentence.
The first one has been done for you.

1. All modern human beings belong to the scientific class of __**Homo sapiens**__. (Root = HOM)

2. Crime scene investigators use modern tools such as DNA analysis to solve _____ cases. (Root = HOM)

3. The _____ had a difficult time getting along with his co-workers. (Root = ANTHROPO)

4. _____ helps explain relationships between people in different cultures around the world. (Root = ANTHROPO)

5. Many private schools rely on _____ to pay for programs such as art, music, and sports. (Root = ANTHROPO)

6. Except for its choppy movements and noisy internal motors, the _____ looked and sounded like a real human being. (Root = ANDRO)

Growing Your Vocabulary: Learning from Latin and Greek Roots

Exercises
Word Bank

Homo sapiens	anthropology	philanthropy
homicide	misanthrope	android

III. Define It! (Part 2)

DIRECTIONS: Based on what you have learned in this chapter, define each of the following in your own words, and create a sentence using the word.

1. homicide: _____

_____

2. Homo sapiens: _____

_____

3. anthropology: _____

_____

4. misanthrope: _____

_____

5. philanthropy: _____

_____

6. android: _____

_____

IV. Personalize It!

DIRECTIONS: Using your understanding of the vocabulary words, respond to the following prompts. Use a separate piece of paper if necessary.

1. If you are an *anthropologist* and were given the money to study one culture, what would you study, and why?

_____

2. There are already many *androids* in development today. What do you believe life will be like when they are able to do more things?

_____

3. Describe the greatest advantage of being part of the *Homo sapiens* species as compared to being an animal or a robot.

_____

4. What do you think is a fair punishment for someone who commits a *homicide*?

_____

Chapter 10:
Exercises

-- *Word Bank* --

Homo sapiens   anthropology   philanthropy
homicide   misanthrope   android

V. Decode It!

DIRECTIONS: Use what you have learned about the words *homo*, *hominis*, the roots *anthropo* and *andro*, and the prefixes and suffixes in this chapter to answer the following questions:

1. *Homo habilis* is an extinct ancestor of *Homo sapiens*. *Habilis* means "skillful." What do you suppose the name *Homo habilis* told us about this species of man?

   _____

   _____

2. Review the prefix *in–*. What do you think it means to be *inhumane* if being humane means that you are compassionate?

   _____

   _____

3. The Latin root *hom* means "human." If you are honored for the charitable work you have done for an organization, you might be described as a *humanitarian*. What type of person are you? What other words might be used to describe you?

   _____

   _____

VI. Analogies!

DIRECTIONS: For each of the vocabulary words in the chapter, complete the analogy.

1. *Biology* is to *biologist* as _____ is to *anthropologist*.

2. *Misers* are to _____ as *violent protestors* are to *peace*.

3. *Steel* and *rubber* are to *cars* as *muscles* and *bones* are to _____.

4. *Creation* is to *life* as _____ is to *death*.

5. *Friendly* is to _____ as *speedy* is to *snail*.

6. *Yell* is to *scream* as _____ is to *robot*.

Growing Your Vocabulary: Learning from Latin and Greek Roots

$\mathscr{Word\ Bank}$

| Homo sapiens | anthropology | philanthropy |
| homicide | misanthrope | android |

VII. Compare It!

DIRECTIONS: One of the techniques for remembering what a word means is to remember a word that is similar in definition (synonym) and a word that is the opposite in definition (antonym). For example, the opposite of the word *humane*, which means compassionate, is *inhumane*. For each of the following vocabulary words, match the word that is most closely the opposite in meaning or the word that means something similar to it. Use the word in parentheses to guide you.

1. homicide (synonym) ___
2. Homo sapiens (synonym) ___
3. philanthropy (antonym) ___
4. android (synonym) ___
5. misanthrope (antonym) ___

A. stinginess
B. people person
C. murder
D. robot
E. human beings

Review It!

DIRECTIONS: Read each question. Then, circle the letter next to the best answer.

1. If you study *anthropology*, you study
   A. weight.
   B. people.
   C. the earth.
   D. animals.
   E. houses.

2. The root of the word *subterranean* means
   A. to hold.
   B. man.
   C. earth.
   D. above.
   E. love.

3. The amount of time Sheila was mayor is called her
   A. lever.
   B. tenure.
   C. pendant.
   D. tenant.
   E. misanthrope.

4. The root in the word *except* comes from the Latin word meaning
   A. to take.
   B. to hang.
   C. to hold.
   D. high.
   E. human being.

5. To make something worse is to _____ it.
   A. relieve
   B. inter
   C. elevate
   D. accept
   E. aggravate

6. Someone who practices *philanthropy*
   A. studies human beings.
   B. likes being in high places.
   C. enjoys being around other people.
   D. reads books.
   E. gives to others.

Review It!

7. The root in the word *homicide* means
    A. man.
    B. to lift.
    C. heaviness.
    D. lightness.
    E. earth.

8. A *misanthrope*
    A. dislikes people.
    B. loves people.
    C. rules people.
    D. fears people.
    E. gives to people.

9. Which of the following comes from the Latin word meaning "to lift"?
    A. android
    B. inter
    C. pendant
    D. lever
    E. gravitate

10. A *tenant* is someone who
    A. gives to people.
    B. holds an office.
    C. lives in a place.
    D. gets something.
    E. likes animals.

11. If you *anticipate* something, you are _____ when it happens.
    A. ready
    B. unaware
    C. sad
    D. away
    E. alive

12. The plane was flying too close to the ground; it needed to gain
    A. altitude.
    B. levity.
    C. philanthropy.
    D. pendulum.
    E. continent.

Review It!

13. An antonym for the word *gravitate* is
    A. enjoy.
    B. avoid.
    C. observe.
    D. write.
    E. lift.

14. The prefix of the word *inter* means
    A. not.
    B. under.
    C. back.
    D. in.
    E. small.

15. You know Pete is in a *pensive* mood because he is
    A. laughing.
    B. dancing.
    C. shouting.
    D. sleeping.
    E. frowning.

16. The root of the word *exalt* means
    A. heavy.
    B. high.
    C. earth.
    D. man.
    E. person.

17. Someone taken prisoner is a(n)
    A. android.
    B. recipient.
    C. captive.
    D. tenant.
    E. misanthrope.

18. A root meaning "man" appears in which of the following?
    A. appendix
    B. homo sapiens
    C. recipient
    D. levity
    E. tenement

Review It!

19. Read the sentence below:

    Felicia didn't want to write a <u>tired, worn-out</u> phrase in the card for Chris.

    Which of the following words is the best synonym for the underlined words?
    A. trite
    B. pensive
    C. grave
    D. pending
    E. subterranean

20. The word that literally means "that which holds together" is
    A. tenure.
    B. intercept.
    C. lever.
    D. continent.
    E. attrition.

21. The suffix of the word *anthropology* means
    A. a person who.
    B. the study of.
    C. full of.
    D. growing.
    E. the killing of.

22. An antonym for the word *alleviate* is
    A. worsen.
    B. relieve.
    C. drop.
    D. intercept.
    E. fly.

23. A gradual loss of people is
    A. philanthropy.
    B. attrition.
    C. homicide.
    D. anthropology.
    E. altitude.

24. Joni is going to jump in front of Francis and _____ the ball.
    A. relieve
    B. captivate
    C. elevate
    D. aggravate
    E. intercept

Artificial

Artisan

Adept

Artifice

Inept

Adapt

Adorn

Apt

Aptitude

Ornate

Growing Your Vocabulary: Learning from Latin and Greek Roots

art

orn

apt/ept

Chapter 11:

Art, the Artist, and Beauty

This chapter is all about words that have to do with beauty and art. "Love of beauty is Taste. The creation of beauty is Art."—RALPH WALDO EMERSON

Roots to Learn:

art	orn
apt/ept	

Words to Learn:

artisan	adapt
artificial	apt
artifice	aptitude
adorn	adept
ornate	inept

Suffix:

–ial

We get our word **ART** from the Latin noun **ARS**, **ARTIS**, which literally means "art." The root **ART** comes from this word.

An **ARTISAN** is a craftsperson, someone who makes art.

It is important not to confuse an artist with an **ARTISAN**. They are not the same. An artisan is a person who works in crafts, like pottery, carpentry, brickworking, textiles, etc. An artist, however, paints, sculpts, dances, writes, directs, etc.

*A skilled **artisan** crafted the clay pots that were sold at the festival.*

Chapter 11:
Art, the Artist, and Beauty

ARTIFICIAL means "created or invented; not natural or genuine."

*Scientists created an **artificial** reef from old car tires.*

In 2007, Florida attempted to create an **ARTIFICIAL** reef out of nearly 2 million tires. However, the attempt was unsuccessful, and the reef had to be removed before it could do permanent damage to the natural coastal ecosystem.

SUFFIX ALARM!
The suffix –*ial* means "having the quality of or relating to."
Example:
president + –*ial* = presidential—of or related to a president

An **ARTIFICE** is a deception or mask.

How do you think the first four words of this chapter are related? They all have the root *art* in them, and they deal with things that are not real. Artists and artisans create artificial realities, and someone using **ARTIFICE** makes something false seem true.

I'VE ALWAYS SUPPORTED THE FREE LUNCH PROGRAM.

THAT'S NOT WHAT YOU SAID LAST YEAR.

*The journalist disapproved of the politician's **artifice**.*

Growing Your Vocabulary: Learning from Latin and Greek Roots

The Latin verb **ORNARE, ORNATUS** means "to decorate." The root **ORN** comes from this word.

ADORN means "to decorate."

Have you ever seen the way some people **ADORN** their pets with ribbons or clothing?

*Flags and banners **adorn** the downtown area on the Fourth of July.*

ORNATE means "highly decorated or intricate."

The difference between these two words, *adorn* and *ornate*, is a difference of amount or of degree. Just because something is adorned does not mean it is ornate. That word also has the extra meaning of "a great deal of decoration." Don't confuse the two.

*The weaver worked the threads into an **ornate** design.*

Growing Your Vocabulary: Learning from Latin and Greek Roots

Chapter 11:
Art, the Artist, and Beauty

The Latin verb **APTARE**, **APTATUS** means "to fit." The root **APT** comes from this word.

To **ADAPT** is to adjust to one's environment.

....

APT means "fitting or suitable."

APT also means "likely." In this sentence,, the word apt is aptly used: "George Washington was apt to be elected because of his leadership during the Revolutionary War."

*George Farmer was **aptly** named, since he grew up to be a farmer. His wife also had a fitting name.*

....

*Students who display an **aptitude** for music can attend the band camp.*

APTITUDE is the suitability for a particular subject or activity.

Everyone has an **APTITUDE** for something that he or she can do better than other people. However, some people, like Ben Franklin, show great aptitude in many fields. He was a politician, author, scientist, inventor, public servant, ambassador, printer, and economist.

Growing Your Vocabulary: Learning from Latin and Greek Roots

There are also several words in which the "a" of *apt* becomes an "e":

INEPT means "not suited for something," "incompetent," or "clumsy."

Just as some people are more adept at some things, they are also **INEPT** at others. Most adults can't ride a bicycle as well as most 6th graders, so the grownups would be considered "inept" at this skill.

*The **inept** circus clown couldn't perform even the simplest tricks.*

*The writer is **adept** at managing all of his subplots and keeping the action going.*

ADEPT means "skillful," which is the opposite of inept.

Don't confuse these three words that all look similar: *adept, adopt, adapt.* You'll encounter "adopt" in Chapter 19, but you already have a pretty good idea of what it means.

adept—skillful
adopt—to choose
adapt—to fit

Exercises
Word Bank

artisan	artifice	ornate	aptitude	inept
artificial	adorn	adapt	adept	apt

I. Define It! (Part 1)

DIRECTIONS: Write the letter of the word from the right column that matches the definition in the left column. The first one has been done for you.

1. a craftsperson **C**   A. inept

2. to adjust to one's environment ___   B. artifice

3. created or invented; not natural or genuine ___   C. artisan

4. an ability or skill at something ___   D. adapt

5. to decorate ___   E. artificial

6. highly decorated; intricate ___   F. ornate

7. not suited for something; clumsy or incompetent ___   G. adept

8. skillful ___   H. aptitude

9. a deception or mask ___   I. adorn

10. fitting or suitable ___   J. apt

II. Finish It!

DIRECTIONS: Using the root, write a word to complete each sentence.
The first one has been done for you.

1. The gym was _____**adorned**_____ with silver and white streamers and balloons for the school dance. (Root = ORN)

2. The tools and machinery left in the workshop showed that a(n) _____ had once worked in the space. (Root = ART)

3. *The Big Sleep* is a(n) _____ title for the movie we watched, which I thought was really boring. (Root = APT)

4. The artist was _____ at drawing lifelike portraits. (Root = EPT)

5. Janie uses _____ sweeteners instead of sugar to reduce the number of calories in her cooking. (Root = ART)

6. Students who play musical instruments frequently have a greater _____ in math. (Root = APT)

7. Children whose families move around a lot must learn to _____ to new schools, teachers, and classmates. (Root = APT)

8. The judge didn't like the _____ of the contestants in the beauty pageant because their makeup looked unnatural and overdone. (Root = ART)

9. The actor's _____ performance left the audience wanting a refund. (Root = EPT)

10. We were impressed by the _____ wallpaper and antique furniture in the governor's mansion. (Root = ORN)

················· **Word Bank** ·················

artisan	artifice	ornate	aptitude	inept
artificial	adorn	adapt	adept	apt

III. Define It! (Part 2)

DIRECTIONS: Based on what you have learned in this chapter, define each of the following in your own words, and create a sentence using the word.

1. artisan: _____
_____

2. artificial: _____
_____

3. artifice: _____
_____

4. adorn: _____
_____

5. ornate: _____
_____

6. adapt: _____
_____

7. apt: _____
_____

8. aptitude: _____
_____

9. inept: _____
_____

10. adept: _____
_____

Chapter 11:
Exercises

Word Bank

artisan	artifice	ornate	aptitude	inept
artificial	adorn	adapt	adept	apt

IV. Unscramble It!

DIRECTIONS: The vocabulary words from the chapter have been scrambled. Using the sentence, figure out which word belongs in the blank. Then, unscramble the letters to write the word correctly.

1. David was very _____ at playing the piano because he had long fingers that helped him hit the keys.
   PAETD

2. Sage loved dogs of all kinds, so the stuffed puppy Marsha gave her was a(n) _____ gift.
   TAP

3. At the crafts fair, we saw the creations of local _____.
   RASNTISA

4. The grandfather clock was engraved with _____ designs and delicate carvings.
   RETNOA

5. The young boy displayed an unusual _____ for mathematics because he could complete all the problems without a calculator.
   DAPTUTIE

6. Because many celebrities object to killing animals, they wear _____ furs instead of real ones.
   IFACILATRI

7. Angel's clumsiness made her a(n) _____ dancer.
   PEITN

8. To survive in the wilderness, chameleons _____ to the environment by changing their appearance.
   DATPA

9. Tanya continued to talk about her friends behind their backs, so they began to think that her apparent friendliness was just a(n) _____.
   TEFIRCAI

10. At the pep rally, balloons, streamers, and signs _____ the walls of the auditorium.
    NORDADE

Growing Your Vocabulary: Learning from Latin and Greek Roots

Word Bank

artisan	artifice	ornate	aptitude	inept
artificial	adorn	adapt	adept	apt

V. Personalize It!

DIRECTIONS: Using your understanding of the vocabulary words, respond to the following prompts. Use a separate piece of paper if necessary.

1. Describe one way you have had to *adapt* to your new classes at the beginning of every school year.

_____

2. Describe an experience in which you have felt *inept*.

_____

3. Describe something you feel you are very *adept* at.

_____

4. Should you ever use *artifice* with your friends?

_____

VI. Decode It!

DIRECTIONS: Use what you have learned about the roots *art*, *orn*, and *apt* and the prefixes and suffixes to answer the following questions:

1. If you add the suffix *–ist* to the root *art*, you get the word *artist*, which is a word that you know. What, therefore, do you think the suffix *–ist* means?

_____
_____

2. The suffix *–ability* means "ability to." What word could we make that means "ability to adjust to a person's environment"?

_____
_____

3. The Latin word *ornare, ornatus* means "to decorate." Explain what the word *ornament* has to do with the word *ornare, ornatus*.

_____
_____

4. Describe what playing basketball *ineptly* might look like.

_____
_____

.... *Word Bank* ....

artisan	artifice	ornate	aptitude	inept
artificial	adorn	adapt	adept	apt

VII. Compare It!

DIRECTIONS: In this chapter, two of the words are antonyms (opposites) of one another. *Adept* means "skillful," and *inept* means "incompetent." For each of the vocabulary words in the chapter, find an antonym. Then, use the word correctly in a sentence.

1. artisan:

_____

_____

2. artificial:

_____

_____

3. artifice:

_____

_____

4. adorn:

_____

_____

5. ornate:

_____

_____

6. adapt:

_____

_____

7. apt:

_____

_____

8. aptitude:

_____

_____

9. adept:

_____

_____

10. adept:

_____

_____

······· *Word Bank* ·······

artisan   artifice   ornate   aptitude   inept
artificial   adorn   adapt   adept   apt

VIII. Graffiti Posters!

DIRECTIONS: You are going to create a poster for each of the roots that you have learned in this chapter. For your poster, begin by writing the Latin root word in the middle of the poster. Then, draw branches from the root word to the related words that you learned in this chapter. For each word, draw a picture to illustrate its meaning. For example, for a word like *adapting*, you could draw a picture that illustrates the idea of "fitting in." You may use any of the new words you learned in this chapter. You may even be able to come up with words on your own!

Dictate

Diction

Indict

Edict

Monologue

Prologue

Contradict

Dialogue

Growing Your Vocabulary: Learning from Latin and Greek Roots

dict

log

Chapter 12:

Speech and its Varieties

A famous writer once said, "Two monologues do not make a dialogue." Have you ever thought about what makes communication with another person important? This chapter is all about words for speaking and speech.

Roots to Learn:	**Words to Learn:**	**Prefixes:**
dict log	dictate contradict indict dialogue diction monologue edict prologue	mono– dia–

The Latin word meaning "to say, to speak" is **DICERE, DICTUS.** Words from this verb's root, **DICT,** include **DICTIONARY** (a book that tells you how to say things) and **PREDICT** (to talk about something before it happens).

To **DICTATE** is to read or say words that someone else will write down.

To **INDICT** means "to formally charge."

INDICT is the only word on this list that has a "silent c" in it. The word rhymes with "in light." Since we live in a country of laws, any person can be charged, or indicted, for a crime, and the prosecution must then try to prove his or her guilt. If an elected official is indicted by a court, he or she can then be *impeached.* Look up what that word means and add it to your vocabulary.

*Today, a grand jury is expected to **indict** the owner of the company for theft.*

Chapter 12:
Speech and its Varieties

DICTION is word choice, clearness, and vocal expression of spoken language.

Do you say what you mean? That's using good **DICTION**! Do you make yourself understood? Good diction! Do you pronounce your words correctly? You know it—Good diction!

*The debate coach told her students to speak clearly and use good **diction**.*

*The king signed an **edict** ruling that citizens could have three-day weekends.*

An **EDICT** is a declaration.

Did You Know?
The edict that started the U.S. Revolutionary War was a declaration from the King of England that there would be a tax of 3 pennies on a pound of tea. This edict led directly to the Boston Tea Party.

CONTRADICT means "to go against" or "to disagree with."

When you were younger, you never disagreed with your teachers or parents, but as you have grown older, you realize that you have good opinions also. This maturity is one thing that lets you **CONTRADICT** grownups.

*The scientist's research **contradicted** the commonly held belief.*

Growing Your Vocabulary: Learning from Latin and Greek Roots

The Greek noun **LOGOS** means "speech." We get the words below from this word:

A **DIALOGUE** is speech between two or more people, or a conversation.

PREFIX ALARM!
The prefix *dia*– means "across," "through," or "between."
Example:
dia– + *meter* (Greek word for "measure") = diameter—the measurement of the distance across the middle of a circle

I AM DETERMINED TO PROVE A VILLAIN AND HATE THE IDLE PLEASURE OF THESE DAYS.

A **MONOLOGUE** is a speech by one person.

PREFIX ALARM!
The prefix *mono*– means "one."
Example: mono– + *tone* = monotone—speech that does not vary in pitch. Someone who speaks in a monotone does not vary his or her voice when speaking.

*After practicing for months, Gordon was able to perform the **monologue** perfectly.*

A **PROLOGUE** is an introductory speech to an artistic work.

In the **PROLOGUE** to Shakespeare's play, *Romeo and Juliet*, the actor not only introduces the characters, he also tells the audience exactly what happens in the play: Romeo and Juliet both die!

PROLOGUE

*The **prologue** of the play introduced the main characters.*

Growing Your Vocabulary: Learning from Latin and Greek Roots

Exercises
Word Bank

indict	dictate	contradict	monologue
diction	edict	dialogue	prologue

I. Define It! (Part 1)

DIRECTIONS: Write the letter of the word from the right column that matches the definition in the left column. The first one has been done for you.

1. a declaration **B**
2. to speak in order for someone to write the words down ___
3. a conversation between two or more people ___
4. to formally charge ___
5. an introductory speech or artistic work ___
6. to go against; to disagree with ___
7. a speech by one person ___
8. how one speaks ___

A. diction
B. edict
C. monologue
D. dialogue
E. indict
F. contradict
G. dictate
H. prologue

II. Finish It!

DIRECTIONS: Using the root, write a word to complete each sentence.
The first one has been done for you.

1. The most recent _____**edict**_____ from the principal stated that boys could not wear their hair below their collars. (Root = DICT)

2. Kendra was proud of herself for remembering all the lines in her _____. It was hard to stay on stage for so long by herself! (Root = LOG)

3. The police didn't know what to do because all the witnesses _____ each other, and no one could agree on what actually happened. (Root = DICT)

4. Even though they knew that Seth had broken into the barn, the community members knew he had a good reason, so they chose not to _____ him. (Root = DICT)

5. The _____ to the play included a song that told about the characters' wedding day ten years before. (Root = LOG)

6. Martin Luther King, Jr., is known for his powerful, passionate words and his superb _____. (Root = DICT)

7. The teacher had a difficult time finding the _____ in Jakob's short story because he forgot to use quotation marks to show that the characters were speaking to one another. (Root = LOG)

8. Heather spoke slowly as she _____ her campaign speech, so Jeff could write it down for the school newspaper. (Root = DICT)

········· **Word Bank** ·········

indict	dictate	contradict	monologue
diction	edict	dialogue	prologue

III. Define It! (Part 2)

DIRECTIONS: Based on what you have learned in this chapter, define each of the following in your own words, and create a sentence using the word.

1. indict: _____

_____

2. diction: _____

_____

3. edict: _____

_____

4. contradict: _____

_____

5. dialogue: _____

_____

6. monologue: _____

_____

7. prologue: _____

_____

8. dictate: _____

_____

·········· *Word Bank* ··········

| indict | dictate | contradict | monologue |
| diction | edict | dialogue | prologue |

IV. Apply It To The Real World!

DIRECTIONS: In this chapter you have learned the definitions of words that deal with speech. You should also know how those words can be applied in the real world. Using the words from the chapter, answer the following questions:

1. Which of the vocabulary words in the chapter describes something a district attorney might do to a criminal, resulting in that criminal's arrest? _____

2. Which of the vocabulary words in the chapter would be used to describe your mother and father having a conversation? _____

3. Which vocabulary word would you use to describe a speech given by a character who is alone on stage? _____

4. Which of the vocabulary words is used to describe the different ways people speak publicly?
   _____

5. Which of the vocabulary words describes something you might do if you disagreed with someone?
   _____

6. Which of the vocabulary words describes something you might find at the beginning of a story?
   _____

7. Which vocabulary word might describe a new curfew set by your town leaders? _____

8. Which of the vocabulary words describes what is happening if you are talking and someone is writing down what you say? _____

·· **Word Bank** ··

indict	dictate	contradict	monologue
diction	edict	dialogue	prologue

V. Decode It!

DIRECTIONS: Use what you have learned about the roots *dict* and *log* and the prefixes and suffixes in this chapter to answer the following questions:

1. Review the prefix *pre–*. What do you think *precaution* means?

_____

_____

2. The suffix *–ist* means "one who studies." What do you think a *zoologist* is?

_____

_____

3. One meaning of the prefix *epi–* is "after." Where would you expect to find an *epilogue* in a book?

_____

_____

4. You know the word *predict*. How does the meaning of the prefix *pre–* and the root *dict* relate to the meaning of *predict*?

_____

_____

VI. Find It!

DIRECTIONS: You were introduced to eight vocabulary words that are formed from the roots *dict* and *log*. However, there are many more words in the English language that use these roots. Using a dictionary, find the definition for the following words that are derived from these roots:

1. benediction: _____

_____

2. indication: _____

_____

3. abdicate: _____

_____

4. epilogue: _____

_____

5. dedicate: _____

_____

········· *Word Bank* ·········

indict   dictate   contradict   monologue

diction   edict   dialogue   prologue

VII. Put It In Context!

DIRECTIONS: For each vocabulary word, write a detailed sentence that explains the meaning of the word through the context of the sentence. You may change the part of speech to fit your sentences.

1. indict:

_____

_____

2. diction:

_____

_____

3. edict:

_____

_____

4. contradict:

_____

_____

5. dialogue:

_____

_____

6. monologue:

_____

_____

7. prologue:

_____

_____

8. dictate:

_____

_____

VIII. Solve It!

DIRECTIONS: Use the clues and words from this chapter to complete the crossword puzzle. Some of the words may be in a different part of speech.

Word Bank

- indict
- diction
- edict
- contradict
- dialogue
- monologue
- prologue
- dictate

Clues:

ACROSS

4. This is a conversation between two people.

5. If you disagree with something a friend says, you might _____ her.

7. The police have to collect a great deal of evidence before they do this.

8. You would find this at the beginning of a play.

DOWN

1. An official statement ordering all citizens to give up their property is an example of this.

2. If only one person is talking for a while, you can say the person is giving one of these.

3. When someone is writing down what you say, you are doing this.

6. If you use sloppy _____, people might misunderstand you.

Unscramble the letters in the circles in the crossword puzzle to make a word that fits in the blanks in the sentence below. The unscrambled word is not one of the vocabulary words from this lesson, but it is related to some of them.

After he read a blog that criticized him rhe angry ___ ___ ___ ___ ___ ___ ___ ___ ruled that no one in his country could use the Internet.

.... *Word Bank* ....

indict	dictate	contradict	monologue
diction	edict	dialogue	prologue

IX. Write About It!

DIRECTIONS: In this chapter, you have learned words about speaking. Write a dialogue that you might have with a friend, parent, or teacher about any topic. Be sure to indicate who is speaking.

_____

_____

_____

_____

_____

_____

_____

_____

_____

Arrogant

Prerogative

Interrogate

Inquisitive

Quest

Query

Acquire

Inquisition

Growing Your Vocabulary: Learning from Latin and Greek Roots

roga

quis

quer

Chapter 13:
Language that Questions

When you were younger, you went through a phase of life called the "questioning phase," when you learned a lot by asking questions about practically everything. In this chapter, you are going to learn words that deal with asking questions.

Roots to Learn:

roga
quer/quisit

Words to Learn:

arrogant	acquire
prerogative	inquisition
interrogate	inquisitive
query	quest

The Latin verb **ROGARE, ROGATUS** means "to ask." **ROGA** is the root that comes from this word. Other words containing the root **ROGA** include:

An **ARROGANT** person is proud and assumes that he or she is more important than others.

If you know someone who is **ARROGANT**, most likely, that person doesn't have many friends. It's very difficult to be close to people who think they are always right or the best!

*We realized how **arrogant** Tina was when she asked the guest of honor to give up his chair for her.*

Chapter 13:
Language that Questions

A **PREROGATIVE** is a right or privilege.

How does the prefix *pre–*, which means "before" or "first," fit into this definition? The answer is that the word **PREROGATIVE** originally meant that someone in ancient Rome's ruling assemblies had the right to speak or vote *before* everyone else. See the connection?

*The customer exercised his **prerogative** to dispute the charges on his bill.*

*The police had a hard time **interrogating** the suspect because he wouldn't answer their questions.*

INTERROGATE means "to question."

"Where did you go?"
"Out."
"Who did you go with?"
"A friend."
"What did you do?"
"Nothing."
"When did you get back?"
"Late."
"Did you get in trouble?"
"I always answer all your questions perfectly. Why do you keep interrogating me?

Growing Your Vocabulary: Learning from Latin and Greek Roots

The Latin verb **QUAERERE**, **QUISITUS** means "to ask." The roots of this word are **QUER** and **QUISIT**.

*The reference librarian fielded dozens of **queries** by e-mail and telephone every day.*

A **QUERY** is a question or a request for information.

"How did the universe begin?" is one **QUERY** that has puzzled scientists and religious scholars for hundreds of years. Maybe someday the answer will be known for sure.

To **ACQUIRE** means "to obtain or get."

Do you want to **ACQUIRE** a college education after high school or go right to work after you graduate? Think about this: The average college graduate earns $52,200 a year, but the average high school graduate earns only $30,400.

*Members of the museum hope to **acquire** more pottery to expand their collection.*

Chapter 13:
Language that Questions

An **INQUISITION** is a formal hearing.

During the famous Spanish Inquisition, which lasted from 1478 to 1834, nearly 20,000 people were executed for crimes against the Catholic Church. Many thousands more were tried, but not sentenced to death.

*During the senate **inquisition**, many senators had to answer questions about the scandal.*

*Some **inquisitive** children followed the photographer around, asking about her camera.*

INQUISITIVE means "asking many questions" or "being curious."

You have learned that *acquire* means "to get." Well, *inquire* means to "to try to get an answer." Therefore, it's easy to see how this new word, **INQUISITIVE**, fits. When you are inquisitive, you are inquiring about things you want answered.

A **QUEST** is a journey to find something.

Just like a question, a **QUEST** is looking for an answer, but a quest usually involves a long and involved search.

*Dr. Chattergee is on a **quest** to discover what happened to King Tut.*

Growing Your Vocabulary: Learning from Latin and Greek Roots

Exercises
Word Bank

arrogant	interrogate	acquire	inquisitive
prerogative	query	inquisition	quest

I. Define It! (Part 1)

DIRECTIONS: Write the letter of the word from the right column that matches the definition in the left column. The first one has been done for you.

1. a journey to find something **C**
2. a choice ___
3. asking many questions; curious ___
4. a formal hearing ___
5. to obtain; to get ___
6. to question ___
7. asking too much; proud ___
8. a question; a request for information ___

A. interrogate
B. inquisition
C. quest
D. arrogant
E. acquire
F. prerogative
G. inquisitive
H. query

II. Finish It!

DIRECTIONS: Using the root, write a word to complete each sentence. The first one has been done for you.

1. We knew our teacher would __**interrogate**__ us about where we had been last period. (Root = ROGA)

2. Kay was so _____ that she thought she knew more than her piano teacher. (Root = ROGA)

3. After the bridge collapsed, the city began a(n) _____ of all the builders and engineers to find who was at fault. (Root = QUISIT)

4. When the researcher could not find the information he needed, he sent a(n) _____ to the Library of Congress for the information. (Root = QUER)

5. In the epic poem *Sir Gawain and the Green Knight*, Sir Gawain must go on a(n) _____ to find the Green Knight exactly one year after their first encounter. (Root = QUER)

6. The _____ little girl exhausted her teacher with all of her questions. (Root = QUISIT)

7. Even if your friends pressure you to make a bad choice, you have the _____ to refuse. (Root = ROGA)

8. In order to become an Eagle Scout, a Boy Scout must _____ 21 merit badges. (Root = QUER)

Chapter 13:
Exercises

Word Bank

arrogant   interrogate   acquire   inquisitive
prerogative   query   inquisition   quest

III. Define It! (Part 2)

DIRECTIONS: Based on what you have learned in this chapter, define each of the following in your own words, and create a sentence using the word.

1. arrogant: _____

_____

2. interrogate: _____

_____

3. acquire: _____

_____

4. inquisitive: _____

_____

5. prerogative: _____

_____

6. query: _____

_____

7. inquisition: _____

_____

8. quest: _____

_____

IV. Personalize It!

DIRECTIONS: Using your understanding of the vocabulary words, respond to the following prompts. Use a separate piece of paper if necessary.

1. Describe a *quest* that you might like to go on some day.

_____

_____

2. What do you think should be done about *arrogant* professional athletes who display bad behavior?

_____

_____

3. Describe something that you would like to have *acquired* by the time you leave middle school.

_____

_____

4. Describe a time when you were able to exercise your own *prerogative*.

_____

_____

Growing Your Vocabulary: Learning from Latin and Greek Roots

Word Bank

arrogant   interrogate   acquire   inquisitive
prerogative   query   inquisition   quest

V. Decode It!

DIRECTIONS: Use what you have learned about the roots *quer*, *quisit*, and *roga* to answer the following questions:

1. Remember that the prefix *in–* means "into." What do you think *inquire* means?

   _____

   _____

2. The word *rogue* describes an immoral, deceitful person. Originally, the word *rogue* referred to a person who pretended to be a beggar and tricked people into donating money. How can the word *rogue* be connected to the root *roga*?

   _____

   _____

3. To *interrogate* is to formally question someone. What do you think an *interrogation* is?

   _____

   _____

4. The Latin word *quaerere*, *quisitus* means "to question." If you are in class and your teacher describes you as *inquisitive*, what other words might be used to describe you?

   _____

   _____

VI. Find It!

DIRECTIONS: You were introduced to eight vocabulary words that are formed from the roots *roga*, *quer*, and *quisit*. However, there are many more words in the English language that use these roots. Using a dictionary, find the definition for the following words that are derived from these roots. Some words have more than one definition, but you should choose the definition that relates most directly to the theme of the chapter.

1. conquistador:

   _____

2. exquisite:

   _____

3. inquest:

   _____

4. prerequisite:

   _____

5. subrogate:

   _____

Chapter 13:
Exercises

Word Bank

arrogant   interrogate   acquire   inquisitive
prerogative   query   inquisition   quest

VII. Compare It! (Part 1)

DIRECTIONS: Many of the words in this chapter have antonyms. For example, the antonym of the word *translucent*, which means "able to be seen through," is *opaque*. Match each of the vocabulary words below to its antonym. Then, match the vocabulary word with its synonym.

Original:	Antonym:	Synonym:
1. arrogant ___	A. give up	F. conceited
2. acquire ___	B. lose	G. pursuit
3. inquisitive ___	C. uninterested	H. question
4. quest ___	D. answer	I. attain
5. query ___	E. modest	J. curious

VIII. Compare It! (Part 2)

DIRECTIONS: Match the vocabulary word with the sentence that uses the correct synonym for the italicized word.

1. The President has the *right* to appoint justices to the Supreme Court. _____

2. At police headquarters, the officer began to *question* the suspect even though his lawyer was not present. _____

3. The *investigation* into origins of the spoiled meat began at the grocery store that sold it to the public. _____

IX. Solve It!

DIRECTIONS: Use the clues and words from this chapter to complete the crossword puzzle. Some of the words may be in a different part of speech.

Word Bank

- arrogant
- prerogative
- interrogate
- query
- acquire
- inquisition
- inquisitive
- quest

Clues:

ACROSS

5. In the story of *King Arthur and the Knights of the Round Table*, King Arthur went on a _____ to save Guinevere.

7. If someone in government needs to find information, the official may begin a formal _____, asking many different people what they know.

8. If you buy a video game that doesn't work and take it back to the store, it's their _____ whether to refund your money or replace the game.

DOWN

1. Young children can often be described as _____ because they ask a lot of questions.

2. If you are asking about something, you are making one of these.

3. Police _____ suspects to gather information.

4. Somebody who is like this probably does not have many friends.

6. When you purchase a gift, you do this.

Unscramble the letters in the circles in the crossword puzzle to make a word that fits in the blanks in the sentence below. The unscrambled word is not exactly from the vocabulary words in this lesson, but it is related to some of them.

During the police ___ ___ ___ ___ ___ ___ ___ ___ ___ ___ ___ ___ ___, an officer asked the suspect many questions.

Chapter 13:
Exercises

·· *Word Bank* ··

arrogant	interrogate	acquire	inquisitive
prerogative	query	inquisition	quest

X. Write About It!

DIRECTIONS: In this chapter, you have learned words about language that we use when we want to question. If you were given the opportunity to ask three questions of someone, whom would you ask, and what questions would you choose?

_____

_____

_____

_____

_____

_____

_____

_____

_____

_____

152
Growing Your Vocabulary: Learning from Latin and Greek Roots

Monarch

Anarchy

Potent

Omnipotent

Impotent

Potentate

Potential

Growing Your Vocabulary: Learning from Latin and Greek Roots

arch

pot

Chapter 14:

Power

Abraham Lincoln once said, "If you want to test a man's character, give him power." What do you think that means about the nature of a person's character? In this chapter, you will learn words that have to do with power.

Roots to Learn:	**Words to Learn:**	**Prefix:**
arch **pot**	monarch potential anarchy potentate potent omnipotent impotent	**omni–**

The Greek verb **ARKHEIN** means "to rule." The root from this word, **ARCH**, forms words having to do with ruling.

A **MONARCH** is a single ruler, usually one who has inherited power because of lineage, such as a king or queen.

ANARCHY is a lack of government.

Did You Know?

Many people know about King Henry VIII. However he was King only a short time. His daughter, Elizabeth I, was Queen for nearly twice as long as Henry was King. But Queen Victoria was England's monarch for 64 years.

*In Japan, the **monarch** is the official head of state, but the prime minister actually leads the government.*

Chapter 14:
Power

The Latin verb **POSSE**, **POTUI** means "to have power" or "to be able."

The root **POT** forms words having to do with power.

A **POTENTATE** is a powerful leader. A monarch is one kind of **POTENTATE**. A dictator is another. Sometimes powerful heads of large companies are also referred to as *potentates*.

*The **potentate** addressed her people once she returned from her visit abroad.*

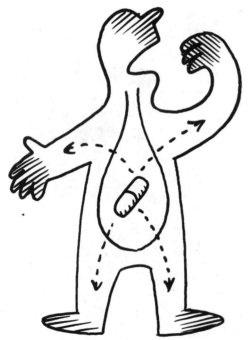

*The **potent** drug began working in minutes.*

POTENT means "very powerful or strong."

Someone who can lift a car, a homerun that sails out of the ball park, a disease that can infect almost anyone, a movie that everyone wants to see, the space shuttle: yes, these can all be described as relating to the word **POTENT**.

Growing Your Vocabulary: Learning from Latin and Greek Roots

IMPOTENT means "not having power."

The prefix *im–*, as you learned in Chapter 2, means "not." Think of the words *impossible, impure,* and *immature.* You should now be able to understand that they mean "not possible," "not pure," and "not mature."

*After losing the tennis match, Maria felt angry, depressed, and **impotent.***

*The newspaper describes this horse as a **potential** Kentucky Derby champion.*

POTENTIAL as an adjective means "about to be" or "able to be."

As a noun, **POTENTIAL** means "capability."

In the United States, anyone can live up to his or her potential, and we all have the potential to be exactly what we want to be. The key is hard work because potential alone doesn't guarantee anything.

*Maurice has the **potential** to be a top salesman.*

Growing Your Vocabulary: Learning from Latin and Greek Roots

Chapter 14:
Power

The word **OMNISCIENT** means "all-knowing."

If you are **OMNIVOROUS**, you will eat all kinds of food: meat, fish, and vegetables, etc.

Did You Know?

You have 3 different types of teeth: Canines (the pointy ones), incisors (the sharp ones in the front), and molars (the flat ones). This shows that people are meant to eat different kinds of food. Grains, like bread, need to be crushed, not cut, but meat needs to be cut. You'd be in real trouble if you had only one kind of tooth in your mouth.

PREFIX ALARM!

The prefix omni– means "all" or "every."
Example:
omni– + present = omnipresent—being everywhere at once

*When it comes to the track team, Coach Jones considers herself practically **omnipotent**.*

OMNIPOTENT means "all-powerful."

Many people in modern society believe in a single **OMNIPOTENT** God, one deity with power over everything, as omnipotent; but it was not always like this. Ancient Greeks had a god for almost everything: One ruled the sea, another the sun, and still another one was in charge of harvests. Some were major gods, but others were much less important.

Growing Your Vocabulary: Learning from Latin and Greek Roots

Exercises

Word Bank

monarch	potent	potential (adjective)	potentate
anarchy	impotent	potential (noun)	omnipotent

I. Define It! (Part 1)

DIRECTIONS: Write the letter of the word from the right column that matches the definition in the left column. The first one has been done for you.

1. all-powerful **D**
2. a single ruler who inherited his or her power ___
3. powerless ___
4. very powerful or strong ___
5. the ability to be ___
6. lack of government ___
7. a powerful leader ___
8. about to be; able to be ___

A. monarch
B. anarchy
C. potentate
D. omnipotent
E. potent
F. impotent
G. potential (adjective)
H. potential (noun)

II. Finish It!

DIRECTIONS: Using the root, write a word to complete each sentence.
The first one has been done for you.

1. The track athletes watched the weather to see if the ____**potential**____ rain shower would arrive in time to disrupt their track meet. (Root = POT)

2. Although the senator's speech was nice, it will be nothing more than _____ words unless he can get other senators to support it. (Root = POT)

3. Queen Elizabeth I was one of the longest-reigning and most successful female _____ in England's history. (Root = ARCH)

4. The newspapers called the mayor "an elected _____ " because she ran the city without asking anyone's advice. (Root = POT)

5. The coffee was so _____ that the waitress had to dilute it with water before it could be served to the customers. (Root = POT)

6. After the experimental eye surgery, the blind man had the _____ to see again. (Root = POT)

7. The United States uses a system of checks and balances to keep any branch of government from acting as if it were _____. (Root = POT)

8. The class erupted in _____ as soon as Mrs. Patterson left the room. (Root = ARCH)

······························· *Word Bank* ·······························

monarch	potent	potential (adjective)	potentate
anarchy	impotent	potential (noun)	omnipotent

III. Define It! (Part 2)

DIRECTIONS: Based on what you have learned in this chapter, define each of the following in your own words, and create a sentence using the word.

1. monarch: _____
_____

2. anarchy: _____
_____

3. potentate: _____
_____

4. omnipotent: _____
_____

5. potent: _____
_____

6. impotent: _____
_____

7. potential (adj.): _____
_____

8. potential (n.): _____
_____

········· *Word Bank* ·········

monarch	potent	potential (adjective)	potentate
anarchy	impotent	potential (noun)	omnipotent

IV. Unscramble It!

DIRECTIONS: The vocabulary words from the chapter have been scrambled. Using the sentence, figure out which word belongs in the blank. Then, unscramble the letters to write the word correctly.

1. The _____ of the country lives in a grand palace far from his subjects.
   TAOPTETNE

2. The straight-A student had the _____ to become anything he wanted in life.
   IPTLANTOE

3. Queen Elizabeth II is probably the most famous living _____; she has been Queen since 1952.
   NAMRHCO

4. Her perfume was so _____ that we could smell it whenever she walked past the door.
   TEPONT

5. The law requiring drivers to wear seatbelts was completely _____ until the police began writing tickets.
   TINTMPEO

6. The town was practically in a state of _____ after the mayor's assassination.
   AYRHACN

7. No mortal person is truly _____—even dictators can't control the weather.
   NPOITENMOT

8. The life preservers and lifeboats were available for use in any _____ emergencies.
   NPLAIOTET

Chapter 14:
Exercises

Word Bank

monarch	potent	potential (adjective)	potentate
anarchy	impotent	potential (noun)	omnipotent

V. Signify It!

DIRECTIONS: On index cards, create a symbol for each of the vocabulary words in this chapter. For example, in the last chapter, you learned the vocabulary word *quest*. If you were going to create a symbol for the word, you might draw a map with an "X" to "mark the spot." Be creative with your symbols, but make sure that you can use the symbol to help you remember the meaning of the word. On the back of the card, write an explanation for how your symbol helps clarify the meaning of the word.

VI. Analogies!

DIRECTIONS: For each of the vocabulary words in the chapter, complete the analogy.

1. _____ is to *possible* as *boring* is to *dull*.

2. *Air* is to *vacuum* as *government* is to _____.

3. *Power* is to _____ as *food* is to *omnivorous*.

4. *Elected* is to _____ as *ocean* is to *desert*.

5. *Moisture* is to *wet* as *powerful* is to _____.

6. *Hide and seek* is to *game* as *queen* is to _____.

7. *Strong* is to _____ as *tiny* is to *enormous*.

8. _____ is to *assured* as *mysterious* is to *known*.

Growing Your Vocabulary: Learning from Latin and Greek Roots

················· *Word Bank* ·················

monarch	potent	potential (adjective)	potentate
anarchy	impotent	potential (noun)	omnipotent

VII. Put It In Context!

DIRECTIONS: Complete the sentence in a way that shows you understand what the vocabulary word in italics means.

1. Because Great Britain has a long-standing *monarchy*,…

_____

2. The *potentate* ruled his subjects by…

_____

3. The boxer had the *potential*…

_____

4. When the country was in a state of *anarchy*,…

_____

5. I am not *omnipotent* because…

_____

6. The government became completely *impotent* when…

_____

7. The doctor needed the most *potent* medicine in order to…

_____

8. One *potential* way to stop the boat from sinking was…

_____

·········· *Word Bank* ··········

| monarch | potent | potential (adjective) | potentate |
| anarchy | impotent | potential (noun) | omnipotent |

VIII. Write About It!

DIRECTIONS: In this chapter, you have learned words about government and power. We live in a democratic republic, but in this chapter you learned about *monarchy* and *anarchy*. Write a paragraph that describes the advantages of living in the kind of government you think is best.

_____

_____

_____

_____

_____

_____

_____

_____

_____

Jurisprudence

Legitimate

Legislate

Justify

Justice

Jurisdiction

Perjure

Growing Your Vocabulary: Learning from Latin and Greek Roots

leg

jus/jur

Chapter 15:

Laws and Justice

We live in a country in which laws are determined by the Constitution of the United States. In this chapter, you are going to learn words that have to do with laws and justice.

Roots to Learn:	Words to Learn:	Suffixes:
leg **jus/jur**	legislate jurisdiction legitimate perjure justice jurisprudence justify	**–ice**

The Latin word for "law" is **LEX, LEGIS**. The root from this word is **LEG**. Words we get from this root include **LEGAL** and **ILLEGAL**, as well as the ones below:

To **LEGISLATE** means "to make into law."

LEGITIMATE is valid or lawful.

When two or more people have a **LEGITIMATE** claim about the same thing, a legal institution, like the courts, must decide which person has the best case. Then, the government may have to **LEGISLATE** a way that makes the case a law. For example, you and a friend might both claim that you own the same land, and you both might have papers showing the land has been in your family for many years. A judge would decide which claim on the land was more legitimate, and your state legislature would write a new law about owning land.

*New Jersey was one of the first states to **legislate** a recycling program.*

Chapter 15:
Laws and Justice

Another Latin word for "law" is **JUS**, **JURIS**. We get words with both **JUS** and **JUR** from this root.

By adding the suffix *–ice* to the root *jus*, we get a word that means "something having qualities of fairness and law."

JUSTICE is the fair administration of law.

As a public defender, Dave has devoted his life to preserving *justice*.

Did You Know?

If a person is charged with a crime and "cannot afford a lawyer, one will be appointed for you." You must have heard that phrase on many TV programs about trials. The reason the courts will appoint a lawyer is to make sure that everyone receives a fair trial, regardless of his or her ability to pay for an attorney.

SUFFIX ALARM!

The suffix *–ice* means "state or condition of" or "activity related to."
Example:
coward + *–ice* = cowardice—a habit or condition of fear

How can Rosa **justify** driving 1,100 miles just to pick up a goldfish?

To **JUSTIFY** is to prove that something is right.

Many people are prejudiced against other people; they **JUSTIFY** disliking an entire group or race because of one or two individuals. This type of behavior just causes more hatred. Trying to justify prejudice is stupid!

Growing Your Vocabulary: Learning from Latin and Greek Roots

A **JURISDICTION** is an area where a law or power of law is in effect.

Did You Know?

Many countries claim they own the parts of the oceans that border their country. In other words, they have jurisdiction over these areas. Some countries have a 20 mile limit, but others claim a 200 mile jurisdiction.

*The accident occurred within the **jurisdiction** of the Bridgeville police.*

I PROMISE TO TELL THE TRUTH.

*Judge Palumbo suspected that the witness was about to **perjure** himself.*

To **PERJURE** is to lie under oath in a court of law.

Why do you think that people have to swear "to tell the truth" in court? That's easy! If there were no oath to take, people could say anything they wanted! The truth could never be found if witnesses could **PERJURE** themselves without fear of going to jail.

JURISPRUDENCE is the science of the law.

Anyone who wants to become a judge or lawyer must study **JURISPRUDENCE**. The word is one of the oldest we know of; it existed as far back as Ancient Rome.

*Naomi is an expert on **jurisprudence** because she graduated with a law degree and passed the bar exam.*

Exercises

Word Bank

legislate	justice	jurisdiction	jurisprudence
legitimate	justify	perjure	

I. Define It! (Part 1)

DIRECTIONS: Write the letter of the word from the right column that matches the definition in the left column. The first one has been done for you.

1. to prove that something is right **G**

2. to make into law ___

3. the science of the law ___

4. the fair administration of law ___

5. an area where a law or power of law is in effect ___

6. to lie under oath ___

7. valid; lawful ___

A. jurisprudence

B. legislate

C. justice

D. jurisdiction

E. perjure

F. legitimate

G. justify

II. Finish It!

DIRECTIONS: Using the root, write a word to complete each sentence.
The first one has been done for you.

1. It's hard to _____**justify**_____ going to a store when you don't need to buy anything. (Root = JUS)

2. Paul Emory Washington had to provide a birth certificate to prove that he was a _____ descendant of George Washington because no one would take his word for it. (Root = LEG)

3. Australia began to _____ the use of seatbelts in 1970, but the United States didn't make wearing seatbelts a law until 1984. (Root = LEG)

4. The two state counties were having a disagreement over the _____ of a local robbery because it happened near the county line. (Root = JUR)

5. In order to become a judge, a candidate must be an expert on _____. (Root = JUR)

6. Most citizens believe that criminals should be punished and that there should be _____ for victims of crimes. (Root = JUS)

7. The attorney thought that the witness was _____ himself, and a lie detector test proved that he was right. (Root = JUR)

Growing Your Vocabulary: Learning from Latin and Greek Roots

Exercises

Word Bank

legislate	justice	jurisdiction	jurisprudence
legitimate	justify	perjure	

III. Define It! (Part 2)

DIRECTIONS: Based on what you have learned in this chapter, define each of the following in your own words, and create a sentence using the word.

1. legislate: _____
_____

2. legitimate: _____
_____

3. justice: _____
_____

4. justify: _____
_____

5. jurisdiction: _____
_____

6. perjure: _____
_____

7. jurisprudence: _____
_____

IV. Personalize It!

DIRECTIONS: Using your understanding of the vocabulary words, respond to the following prompts. Use a separate piece of paper if necessary.

1. Explain the *legislative* branch of the government. What does this branch do?
_____
_____

2. People who are testifying in a court of law might *perjure* themselves and not tell the truth. What do you think should be the punishment for this offense?
_____
_____

3. What is a *legitimate* reason for you to miss a day of school?
_____
_____

4. Write about a time when you have had to *justify* yourself or your actions to your friends or family.
_____
_____

Chapter 15:
Exercises

.... *Word Bank* ....

legislate	justice	jurisdiction	jurisprudence
legitimate	justify	perjure	

V. Decode It!

DIRECTIONS: Use what you have learned about the roots *leg*, *jus*, and *jur* and the prefixes and suffixes in this chapter to answer the following questions:

1. Review the prefix *in–*. What do you think *injustice* is?

   _____

   _____

2. The Latin word *judicia* is related to *jus, juris* and means "judgment." What is the purpose of the *judicial* branch of the United States government?

   _____

   _____

3. What verb do you get when you add the prefix *in–*, meaning "not," to the *jur* root? What does this verb mean?

   _____

   _____

4. The Latin root *pen* means "punishment or penalty." If you break a law, you will be penalized. What do you think a *penitentiary* is?

   _____

   _____

VI. Find It!

DIRECTIONS: You were introduced to seven vocabulary words that are formed from the roots *leg*, *jus*, and *jur*. However, there are many more words in the English language that use these roots. Using a dictionary, find the definition for the following words that are derived from these root words. Some words have more than one definition, but you should choose the definition that relates most directly to the theme of the chapter.

1. legalize: _____

2. conjure: _____

3. privilege: _____

4. illegitimacy: _____

5. extralegal: _____

Growing Your Vocabulary: Learning from Latin and Greek Roots

········· *Word Bank* ·········

legislate	justice	jurisdiction	jurisprudence
legitimate	justify	perjure	

VII. Put It In Context!

DIRECTIONS: Complete the sentence in a way that shows you understand what the vocabulary word in italics means.

1. The city council had to *legislate*…

_____

_____

2. A *legitimate* excuse for not having your homework done on time is not…

_____

_____

3. *Justice* was served when…

_____

_____

4. The fact that the air conditioner was broken *justified*…

_____

_____

5. The crime was outside the officer's *jurisdiction*…

_____

_____

6. The witness *perjured* herself and…

_____

_____

7. A degree in *jurisprudence*…

_____

_____

Word Bank

legislate	justice	jurisdiction	jurisprudence
legitimate	justify	perjure	

VIII. Write About It!

DIRECTIONS: In this chapter you have learned words about law and justice. Write about a time when you felt that you were treated *unjustly*. What do you believe the outcome should have been in your situation?

_____

_____

_____

_____

_____

_____

_____

_____

_____

Review It!

DIRECTIONS: Read each question. Then, circle the letter next to the best answer.

1. Which word best completes the sentence below?

    In the _____, the writer explains what the story is going to be about.

    A. aptitude
    B. prologue
    C. indict
    D. adorn
    E. contradict

2. Which of the following words means "made up" or "not real"?
    A. artificial
    B. justice
    C. diction
    D. jurisprudence
    E. impotent

3. A synonym for *powerful* is
    A. potent.
    B. acquire.
    C. artisan.
    D. arrogant.
    E. quest.

4. Which of the following words has a prefix meaning "all"?
    A. monarch
    B. prologue
    C. contradict
    D. jurisprudence
    E. omnipotent

5. Which word best completes the sentence below?

    Helene tried to _____ her odd actions to Dave.

    A. adorn
    B. indict
    C. acquire
    D. perjure
    E. justify

6. Which of the following words means the same thing as "decorate"?
    A. adorn
    B. adapt
    C. dictate
    D. perjure
    E. contradict

Review It!

7. Which of the following words comes from the Latin word meaning "law"?
   A. dictate
   B. artificial
   C. monarch
   D. legislate
   E. query

8. The Latin root meaning "to ask" appears in the word
   A. anarchy.
   B. justice.
   C. potential.
   D. dialogue.
   E. quest.

9. A word meaning "to lie under oath" is
   A. query.
   B. adorn.
   C. perjure.
   D. legislate.
   E. acquire.

10. The prefix in the word *contradict* means
    A. before.
    B. against.
    C. inside.
    D. towards.
    E. under.

11. A word that means the same thing as *conversation* is
    A. potentate.
    B. monarch.
    C. dialogue.
    D. quest.
    E. potential.

12. Which of the following words comes from the Greek word meaning "to rule"?
    A. monarch
    B. legislate
    C. artisan
    D. diction
    E. prologue

Review It!

13. Which of the following words means "too proud"?
    A. arrogant
    B. artificial
    C. impotent
    D. legitimate
    E. ornate

14. Which word best completes the sentence below?

    One picture frame was plain wood; the other was covered in _____ carvings.

    A. inquisitive
    B. ornate
    C. arrogant
    D. potent
    E. artificial

15. Which word describes someone who is very skillful?
    A. adept
    B. inquisitive
    C. potent
    D. legitimate
    E. omnipotent

16. Another word for "style of speaking" is
    A. anarchy.
    B. query.
    C. artisan.
    D. aptitude.
    E. diction.

17. The word *inept* means the same thing as
    A. made-up.
    B. clumsy.
    C. all-powerful.
    D. pretty.
    E. curious.

18. A person who creates things is a(n)
    A. anarchy.
    B. artisan.
    C. jurisdiction.
    D. monarch.
    E. prologue.

Review It!

19. Which of the following words comes from the Latin word meaning "to fit"?
    A. legislate
    B. justice
    C. artificial
    D. apt
    E. indict

20. Which word would be used for something that could happen?
    A. potential
    B. omnipotent
    C. artificial
    D. legitimate
    E. adept

21. The Latin root meaning "to speak" appears in the word
    A. artisan.
    B. potential.
    C. dictate.
    D. monarch.
    E. adorn.

22. Which of the following words is most likely to be used in a court of law?
    A. indict
    B. adapt
    C. adorn
    D. acquire
    E. dictate

23. The word *query* comes from the Latin root meaning
    A. power.
    B. to ask.
    C. law.
    D. to fit.
    E. art.

24. A *potentate* is a(n)
    A. area where laws are active.
    B. short speech.
    C. lawmaker.
    D. person who makes crafts.
    E. ruler.

Verify

Veracity

Fidelity

Confidant

Infidel

Verdict

Confide

Growing Your Vocabulary: Learning from Latin and Greek Roots

ver

fid

Chapter 16:

Truth and Faith

The motto of the Marine Corps is "Semper Fidelis," which means "Always Faithful." In this chapter, you are going to learn words that deal with truth and faith.

INNOCENT OR GUILTY?

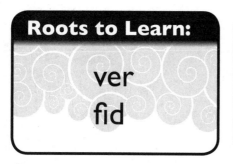

Roots to Learn:

ver

fid

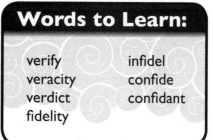

Words to Learn:

verify　　infidel
veracity　confide
verdict　　confidant
fidelity

The Latin word meaning "true" is **VERUS**. We get the root **VER** from this word.

To **VERIFY** means "to check the truth of something."

President Ronald Reagan once said about a treaty that the U.S. should "trust but verify!" What do you think that statement means? Is there any sense in trusting something if you cannot **VERIFY** it?

I SAW TWELVE RACCOONS RUN INTO THE CAFETERIA!

SCHOOL PAPER

*The reporter had to **verify** the facts of her story by talking to other witnesses.*

Chapter 16:
Truth and Faith

VERACITY means "truth."

Aliens? Bigfoot? The Loch Ness Monster? Ghosts?
Chupacabra? Many people believe in these mysterious
creatures. However, to prove the **VERACITY** of the claims
that these things exist, some proof must be shown, but, so far,
no clear evidenxe has ever been produced.

Many letters to the editor questioned
the *veracity* of the article.

It took the jury five days to agree on a *verdict*.

Remember that the root *dict* means "to say."

A **VERDICT** is a statement of guilt or innocence.

Many people do not want to be on a jury because they
don't want the responsibility of determining a verdict that
could send someone to prison. However, very few people
have any problems voting for the verdict on a reality show.

Growing Your Vocabulary: Learning from Latin and Greek Roots

The Latin adjective **FIDUS** means "faithful." The related verb **FIDERE** means "to trust or to believe." The root that comes from these words is **FID**.

FIDELITY means "faithfulness."

Have you ever met a sports fan who has enormous **FIDELITY** to a favorite team? These people decorate their homes in team colors, paint their faces when they go to games, and feel horrible if the team loses. They are showing their faith in almost everything they do.

The lieutenant served her country with *fidelity* and honor.

Surprisingly, the man everybody thought was an *infidel* studied religion in his spare time.

INFIDEL means "a nonbeliever" or "someone who betrays."

Many wars have been fought, and many millions, yes millions, of people have been killed because they were supposedly **INFIDELS**. The Salem Witch Trials, The Crusades, The Spanish Inquisition, and other examples of persecution have occured throughout history.

CONFIDE means "to trust someone with information."

How do you think that the word **CONFIDE** relates to faith. That's easy to explain. The prefix *con–* means "with." Therefore, confide literally means "with faith." You want to *confide* in someone who you trust with the information.

*Vickie **confided** to Jane that she had a crush on Tom.*

*Mary has been my main **confidant** for many years.*

A **CONFIDANT** is someone to whom you can tell something private without fearing that he or she will tell anyone else.

Do not confuse this word, **CONFIDANT**, with the adjective that means being sure of something—*confident*. The two words certainly are related: A confidant is someone you are confident will not betray you.

Exercises
Word Bank

verify	verdict	infidel	confidant
veracity	fidelity	confide	

I. Define It! (Part 1)

DIRECTIONS: Write the letter of the word from the right column that matches the definition in the left column. The first one has been done for you.

1. to check the truth of something **B**
2. someone who can keep a secret ___
3. to trust someone with information ___
4. truthfulness ___
5. a betrayer ___
6. a statement of guilt or innocence ___
7. faithfulness ___

A. verdict
B. verify
C. fidelity
D. confidant
E. confide
F. veracity
G. infidel

II. Finish It!

DIRECTIONS: Using the root, write a word to complete each sentence. The first one has been done for you.

1. My grandmother's closest _____**confidant**_____ was my grandfather; they had been married for almost 50 years. (Root = FID)

2. The drummer proved his _____ to his band mates by turning down an offer from a more famous group. (Root = FID)

3. After discussing the facts of the case for seven hours, the jury returned a(n) _____ for the plaintiff. (Root = VER)

4. Jeff discovered that _____ in his sister about getting a detention was a mistake because she told their parents about it the next day. (Root = FID)

5. Felicia did not question the _____ of the statement Paulo made under oath. (Root = VER)

6. The cashier needed to _____ the customer's identity by checking his driver's license. (Root = VER)

7. Henry and Alberto called Marcel a(n) _____ after he joined the other neighborhood's baseball team. (Root = FID)

.... *Word Bank* ....

verify	verdict	infidel	confidant
veracity	fidelity	confide	

III. Define It! (Part 2)

DIRECTIONS: Based on what you have learned in this chapter, define each of the following in your own words, and create a sentence using the word.

1. verify: _____

_____

2. veracity: _____

_____

3. verdict: _____

_____

4. fidelity: _____

_____

5. infidel: _____

_____

6. confide: _____

_____

7. confidant: _____

_____

IV. Personalize It!

DIRECTIONS: Using your understanding of the vocabulary words, respond to the following prompts. Use a separate piece of paper if necessary.

1. Describe a *confidant* of yours. Why do you trust this person so much?

_____

_____

2. Do people *confide* in you? Why or why not?

_____

_____

3. Write about a time when you have had to question the *veracity* of someone's statement. How did it make you feel to have to do that?

_____

_____

4. How important is *fidelity* in your relationship with your friends?

_____

_____

.... *Word Bank* ....

verify	verdict	infidel	confidant
veracity	fidelity	confide	

V. Decode It!

DIRECTIONS: Use what you have learned about the roots *ver* and *fid* and the prefixes and suffixes in this exercise to answer the questions below:

1. The word *fiancé* means "a man to whom you are engaged," while *fiancée* means "a woman to whom you are engaged." These words come from the *fid* root. How do you think they relate to the root?

   _____

   _____

2. Review the prefix *con–* and the suffix *–ial*. Would you read something you found that was marked *confidential*? Why or why not?

   _____

   _____

3. The Latin prefix *dis–* means "not." The word *diffident* is made up of the prefix *dis–* and the root *fid*. What does it mean if a person is *diffident*?

   _____

   _____

4. The Latin word *bonus* means "good." If a salesperson tries to sell you something and says that it is a *bona fide* offer, should you buy it? What does *bona fide* mean?

   _____

   _____

···························· *Word Bank* ····························

verify   verdict   infidel   confidant

veracity   fidelity   confide

VI. Compare It!

DIRECTIONS: Find a synonym from the word bank for each *italicized* word or phrase in the following sentences:

1. The *non-believer* did not agree with the group's faith. _____

2. Ramon's *trusted companion*, Irena, betrayed him by sharing his secret with the whole school.
   _____

3. The spy challenged the scientist's *allegiance* to his nation by offering him large amounts of cash in exchange for secrets. _____

4. Guards *authenticate* the identity of every person who enters the maximum-security vault.
   _____

5. Jennifer knew she could *admit* to Jason that she had told the teacher who cheated on the test.
   _____

6. The judge's *ruling* was not popular among the people in the courtroom. _____

7. The scientist was able to judge the *accuracy* of the lab test by checking the results against other tests.
   _____

VII. Solve It!

DIRECTIONS: Use the words from this chapter as clues to complete the crossword puzzle. The answers in the puzzle will be synonyms for the vocabulary words.

Word Bank

- decision
- faithfulness
- friend
- honesty
- prove
- reveal
- unbeliever

Clues:

ACROSS

1. confidant

5. fidelity

6. confide

7. veracity

DOWN

2. infidel

3. verify

4. verdict

Unscramble the letters in the circles in the crossword puzzle to answer the question below. The unscrambled word is not exactly from the vocabulary words in this lesson, but it is related to some of them.

What word means something you have when you are sure of your abilities?

— — — — — — — — **C** —

·· *Word Bank* ··

verify	verdict	infidel	confidant
veracity	fidelity	confide	

VIII. Write About It!

DIRECTIONS: In this chapter you have learned words about truth and faith. If you had to explain *veracity* to a child, what would you compare it with so he or she would understand the concept? Write a few sentences in which you explain the importance of *veracity* to a kindergartner. Keep in mind that the words you use should be suitable for a kindergartner's education level and experience.

_____

_____

_____

_____

_____

_____

_____

_____

Consequence

Sequel

Sequence

Rationale

Subsequent

Ratio

Rational

Ration

Growing Your Vocabulary: Learning from Latin and Greek Roots

sequ

rat

Chapter 17:

Order, Proportion, and Comparison

You are in sixth grade. Last year you were in fifth grade, and next year, you will be in seventh grade. You are following a series of classes in your education. In this chapter you will learn words that have to do with order, proportion, and comparison.

Roots to Learn:

sequ
rat

Words to Learn:

sequence	ratio
sequel	ration
consequence	rational
subsequent	rationale

The Latin word **SEQUOR**, **SECUTUS** means "to follow." From this word we get the root **SEQU**.

SEQUENCE means "order."

Most things in life, in nature, and in the world of business occur in a certain **SEQUENCE**. You are born, you learn to walk, you ride a bike, you learn to drive a car. Spring, summer, fall, winter. A magazine photographer takes a picture, downloads it to the computer, stores it in a file, then prints it out. As you can see, if you were to take a step out of sequence, or put the things in a different order, everything would be wrong! If summer followed winter immediately, the trees would die, your clothes would be all wrong, and Christmas vacation would be right after Labor Day.

A **SEQUEL** is a book, story, or movie that follows another.

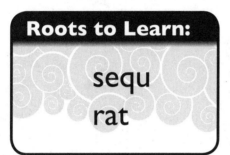

ANTIETAM
FREDERICKSBURG
CHANCELLORSVILLE
VICKSBURG
GETTYSBURG

*The students were asked to list the Civil War battles in the **sequence** in which they occurred.*

Have you seen or read any famous sequels? With some, it's difficult to tell which was the original. Look at this list of movies and see if you can figure out the sequence of the sequels: *Frankenstein Reborn, Frankenstein, Frankenstein and Me, Frankenweenie, Frankenstein's Daughter, Bride of Frankenstein.*

Chapter 17:
Order, Proportion, and Comparison

A **CONSEQUENCE** is a result that follows an action.

Every action has **CONSEQUENCES**. Sometimes, there are what's called "unintended consequences," which means that what happens is not expected. For example, a boy might start smoking cigarettes because he thinks that smoking is cool. After a few years, the boy can't run as far as he could before, he gets sick easier than before, and he has really horrible breath. These are the unintended consequences of trying to be cool. We won't even mention the terrible diseases that smoking can cause!

*The poor crop yield was a **consequence** of the drought.*

....

SUBSEQUENT means "coming after in time" or "following."

NO PROBLEM!

*Solving the complex math problem made **subsequent** problems seem much easier.*

SUBSEQUENT to graduating from high school, what do you want to do: go to work or go to college?

Did You Know?

If you are below the primary level of a building, you are at the *sublevel*. If you are in a *submarine*, you can travel under the water. If you are not an authority figure, you are considered a *subordinate*. If your writing is not good enough, it is *substandard*.

Growing Your Vocabulary: Learning from Latin and Greek Roots

The Latin noun **RATIO**, **RATIONIS** means "computation" or "reason." From the root **RAT**, we get words having to do with order and reason.

A **RATIO** is a comparison in size between one thing and another.

What is the **RATIO** of boys to girls in your class? If there are 13 boys and 15 girls, the ratio is 13 to 15. How about the ratio between a dollar and a nickel? That's 100 to 5 or 20 to 1. If you get five A's and two B's on your report card, what's that ratio? Ratios help explain the relationship between many things!

*The **ratio** of the boat to the model is 10:1.*

*During the First World War, the family saved its **ration** of sugar to bake a cake.*

A **RATION** is a calculated portion, and as a verb, it also means "to give a portion."

During certain times of shortages, like major wars, the United States has had to **RATION** various items. During the Second World War, people were given government stamps that allowed them to buy small amounts of rubber, sugar, butter, baby foods, gasoline, cotton, meat, and many other ordinary supplies that are easy to buy today. The rest of the country's supply of these things went to fight the war. For example, most cars were allowed only four gallons of gas each week!!! One stamp allowed a family to buy five pounds of sugar, but the sugar had to last 3 ½ months!!! Can you imagine the hardships this rationing must have caused?

Chapter 17:
Order, Proportion, and Comparison

RATIONAL means "having reason." (The opposite is **IRRATIONAL**.)

You have two areas in your brain—one part controls your emotional responses like anger, love, friendliness, etc.—and another part controls your rational behavior like knowledge, conscious thought, etc. It's when the two mix that trouble begins. You know there's no monster in your closet, but you're frightened when you hear a sound, you know you should study for the test, but you want to play with your friends. As you grow up, your emotions still are going to be strong, but the rational part of your life will take control of most of what you do.

BUILT LIKE A TANK.

BORROW LESS FROM THE BANK.

*When buying a car, try to make as **rational** a decision as possible.*

IT'S ALSO A GOOD PLACE TO DISPLAY MY COLLECTIBLE FIGURINES.

*Greg's **rationale** for keeping his old computer is that the new one might not work properly.*

RATIONALE is a person's reason for doing something. Usually it gives an explanation for the person's actions.

One way to remember the meaning of **RATIONALE** is a simple synonym: an excuse. If I cross the street on a red light, my rationale might be that I'm in a hurry. That's really just a made-up reason, a justification, an excuse.

Growing Your Vocabulary: Learning from Latin and Greek Roots

Exercises
Word Bank

sequence	consequence	ratio	rational
sequel	subsequent	ration	rationale

I. Define It! (Part 1)

DIRECTIONS: Write the letter of the word from the right column that matches the definition in the left column. The first one has been done for you.

1. a book that follows another **F**

2. a comparison in size between one thing and another ___

3. having reason ___

4. the order of something ___

5. a reason for doing something ___

6. a result of an action ___

7. coming after, following ___

8. a calculated portion ___

A. consequence

B. rationale

C. sequence

D. ratio

E. rational

F. sequel

G. subsequent

H. ration

II. Finish It!

DIRECTIONS: Using the root provided, write a word to complete each sentence.
The first one has been done for you.

1. To create a timeline for a novel, you will need to put the main events in the _____**sequence**_____ in which they occur. (Root = SEQU)

2. On the island, the survivors had to _____ the remaining bottles of water so they would not run out before they were rescued. (Root = RAT)

3. Susie's _____ for buying the expensive bicycle was that she earned plenty of money mowing lawns. (Root = RAT)

4. The author will probably write a _____ if his first novel is a success. (Root = SEQU)

5. Leaving the car windows open was not a _____ decision, because it was clearly about to rain! (Root = RAT)

6. After you have used a paint primer on a wall, the _____ step will be to paint the wall with several coats of the desired paint color. (Root = SEQU)

7. The state of Vermont has the largest _____ of cows to people in the entire country. (Root = RAT)

8. As a _____ of riding the roller coaster four times in a row, Mario got dizzy and threw up. (Root = SEQU)

Word Bank

sequence	consequence	ratio	rational
sequel	subsequent	ration	rationale

III. Define It! (Part 2)

DIRECTIONS: Based on what you have learned in this chapter, define each of the following in your own words, and create a sentence using the word.

1. sequence: _____

   _____

2. sequel: _____

   _____

3. consequence: _____

   _____

4. subsequent: _____

   _____

5. ratio: _____

   _____

6. ration: _____

   _____

7. rational: _____

   _____

8. rationale: _____

   _____

IV. Decode It!

DIRECTIONS: Use what you have learned about the roots *sequ* and *rat* and the prefixes and suffixes you have learned to answer the following questions:

1. Review the prefix *pre–*. What do you think a *prequel* is?

   _____

2. If someone asks you to list *consecutive* numbers, what answer would you give?

   _____

3. Review the prefix *ir–*. If someone is being *irrational*, what might you expect that person to be doing?

   _____

4. If the Latin root *sequ* means "to follow," what do you think the Latin term *non sequitur* means? Explain your thinking.

   _____

.... *Word Bank* ....

sequence	consequence	ratio	rational
sequel	subsequent	ration	rationale

V. Unscramble It!

DIRECTIONS: The vocabulary words from the chapter have been scrambled. Using the sentence, figure out which word belongs in the blank. Then, unscramble the letters to write the word correctly.

1. The _____ of boys to girls in the class was three to one.
   ITORA

2. When the electricity went out, the family had to _____ their ten candles because they did not know when the power would come on.
   ONARIT

3. Dialing the correct _____ of numbers will unlock the safe.
   UCEQESEN

4. The outbreak of malaria was one unexpected _____ of the ban on spraying mosquito poison.
   ECUQENESOCN

5. It seemed totally _____ that Treana wanted to take an ice cold shower; the thermometer was at ninety-nine degrees. **ONARLATI**

6. Although the first chapter of the novel was boring, the _____ chapters had me on the edge of my seat!
   QTEBSUNSEU

7. Ashley loved the new romance novel so much that she could not wait for its _____.
   EUSLQE

8. Mrs. Clark's _____ for buying the car was that it was the last one left in her favorite color. **IONATLERA**

Word Bank

sequence	consequence	ratio	rational
sequel	subsequent	ration	rationale

VI. Compare It!

DIRECTIONS: Learning a word's synonym can help you understand the word better. Match each vocabulary word below with a word that has a similar meaning.

1. consecutive ___
2. proportion ___
3. arrangement ___
4. explanation ___
5. continuation ___
6. after-effect ___
7. logical ___
8. allowance ___

A. consequence
B. rationale
C. sequence
D. ratio
E. rational
F. sequel
G. subsequent
H. ration

VII. Solve It!

Directions: Use the clues and words from this chapter to complete the crossword puzzle. The clues you see will be examples or instances of how the word is commonly used.

Word Bank

- sequence
- sequel
- consequence
- subsequent
- ratio
- ration
- rational
- rationale

Clues:

ACROSS

3. the only way to make one loaf of bread feed thirty castaways

6. Seventh grade English follows sixth grade English.

7. using "I bought a new pair of shoes, and now I need a dress to match" as a reason to go shopping

8. losing your computer privileges because you used it without permission

DOWN

1. raking cover in a basement during a tornado instead of watching it from the front porch

2. the second of two of Paul Zindel's books: *The Pigman* and *The Pigman's Legacy*

4. three to one

5. The Civil War came first, then two World Wars and then the War in Iraq.

Unscramble the letters in the circles in the crossword puzzle to answer the question below. The unscrambled word is not exactly from the vocabulary words in this lesson, but it is related to some of them.

If you behave or act without thinking something through, you are acting

— — — — — — — — — — **Y** .

Chapter 17:
Exercises

Word Bank

sequence	consequence	ratio	rational
sequel	subsequent	ration	rationale

VIII. Write About It!

DIRECTIONS: Many popular books and movies are arranged in a series, with one part leading into the next. Using as much vocabulary from this chapter as possible, write a review of a recent TV, movie, or book series that you have seen or read. When writing your review, explain the *rationale* for your opinion; be sure to support it with reasons and examples.

_____

_____

_____

_____

_____

_____

_____

_____

_____

_____

Growing Your Vocabulary: Learning from Latin and Greek Roots

Memorandum

Amnesty

Amnesia

Psychic

Psyche

Commemorate

Psychology

Memorial

Growing Your Vocabulary: Learning from Latin and Greek Roots

psych

memor

mnem

Chapter 18:
Mind Your Memory

Have you ever had problems trying to remember information while taking a test? This chapter is all about words that have to do with the mind and remembering.

Roots to Learn:

psych   memor
mnem

Words to Learn:

psyche   amnesia
psychic   commemorate
psychology   memorandum
amnesty   memorial

The Greek word **PSYCHE** means "mind." From this word we get the root **PSYCH**.

The **PSYCHE** is the mind or the soul.

In Greek mythology, Psyche is the goddess of the soul. She symbolizes the way in which every experience, good or bad, shapes us.

Many people believe that human beings have a psyche or a soul. Others believe that people have nothing spiritual about them. The first group thinks that when a human being dies, part of that person, his or her psyche, lives on; the second group believes that death ends everything. What are your feelings about this?

*Dreams can reveal some of the mysteries of a person's **psyche**.*

PSYCHIC means "to be able to read another's mind," "to predict the future," or "to have powers beyond the laws of nature."

Did You Know?

Many people do not believe in the power of mind-reading. For years, people have claimed to have this kind of power, but most have been caught cheating. A man named James Randi has offered a one million dollar prize to anyone who can prove he or she has psychic ability.

Some people believe in the power to read minds, but others think there's no such thing as **psychic** *abilities.*

The filmmaker made a documentary about the **psychology** *of artists, actors, and musicians.*

PSYCHOLOGY is the study of the mind.

Have you ever heard of the famous doctor, Sigmund Freud? He was an Austrian doctor who quickly came to realize that almost all human behavior had its roots in the human mind. His idea was to have patients talk to him about their lives, their emotions, and their dreams, and then Freud could understand their psyches. It was this idea that simply by talking, people could be cured of many mental diseases that caused him to be known as the "father of **PSYCHOLOGY**."

Growing Your Vocabulary: Learning from Latin and Greek Roots

The Greek word **MIMNESKEIN** means "to remember," and the word **MNEMON** means "remembering." The root **MNEM** comes from these words.

AMNESTY is an official pardon for a wrongdoing.
AMNESTY is a kind of "official forgetting" of a crime.

There are many issues in America that are difficult to resolve. One major controversy is over amnesty for illegal immigrants—people who enter the United States illegally. Should they be granted amnesty and be allowed to stay, or should they be sent back to their own countries?

*The informant agreed to testify if she received **amnesty** for her part in the crime.*

*Patrick felt like he had **amnesia**—he couldn't remember anything he had studied the night before.*

AMNESIA is a loss of memory.

The word **AMNESIA** and almost all other words with this odd letter combination of *–mn–* refers to remembering. A few people have what is called a "photographic memory," which means they can recall things—frequently, very complicated things—after seeing them only once. People who have this talent can remember every word on every page of a book, can memorize a phone book, can remember what day of the week a certain date was, can recall hundreds of names after hearing them once, and many other feats of memory that other people would think are impossible.

Chapter 18:
Mind Your Memory

The Latin noun **MEMOR, MEMORIS** means "remembering." Many words are formed by its root **MEMOR**.

To **COMMEMORATE** is to celebrate or officially remember something or someone.

Here's your chance to find out some little-known information. What holiday is your favorite? Look it up in an encyclopedia, in the library, or online and see what the day actually **COMMEMORATES**.

*Veteran's Day is a holiday that **commemorates** the men and women who fought in wars for our country.*

A **MEMORANDUM** is a written reminder or message.

A short way to refer to a **MEMORANDUM** is by calling it a "memo." Both words simply mean "a short note or reminder." By the way, don't confuse the last two syllables of *memorandum* with the actual word *random*. They have nothing in common!

*According to the **memorandum**, students who fail to turn in their textbooks will be billed for the cost of the book.*

A **MEMORIAL** is something that serves as a reminder or tribute.

Washington, D.C., is sometimes called a "city of monuments" because there are so many buildings that honor famous Americans. A few of the most famous are the Jefferson, Lincoln, and Washington **MEMORIALS** that pay respect to three of the greatest Presidents. The city also has memorials to the Vietnam War, to African-Americans, to veterans, to women, to the Holocaust, and many, many others. You could spend weeks there just looking over the many memorials.

Growing Your Vocabulary: Learning from Latin and Greek Roots

Exercises
Word Bank

psyche	psychology	amnesia	memorandum
psychic	amnesty	commemorate	memorial

I. Define It! (Part I)

DIRECTIONS: Write the letter of the word from the right column that matches the definition in the left column. The first one has been done for you.

1. loss of memory **E**

2. able to read minds ___

3. a written reminder or message ___

4. an official pardon or forgetting of a wrongdoing ___

5. the study of the mind ___

6. the mind or soul ___

7. to celebrate or officially remember something or someone ___

8. something that serves as a reminder or tribute ___

A. psychology

B. memorial

C. psyche

D. memorandum

E. amnesia

F. amnesty

G. psychic

H. commemorate

II. Finish It!

DIRECTIONS: Using the root, write a word to complete each sentence.
The first one has been done for you.

1. The woman stricken with _____**amnesia**_____ was lucky to have her wallet containing her identification card and home address. (Root = MNEM)

2. If you had _____ powers, you might be able to know what other people were thinking. (Root = PSYCH)

3. A person's book and music collection can reveal a lot about his or her _____. (Root = PSYCH)

4. Congress passed a law that granted _____ to certain immigrants and allowed them to live and work in the United States legally. (Root = MNEM)

5. The African American Civil War Museum and Monument in Washington, D.C., _____ the African American struggle for freedom in the United States. (Root = MEMOR)

6. After the longtime community volunteer died, people at the center created a(n) _____ filled with photos and stories about her to remember her good deeds. (Root = MEMOR)

7. Some people study _____ to understand how people behave. (Root = PSYCH)

8. The principal sent a(n) _____ to his staff to remind them of the after-school meeting. (Root = MEMOR)

··· *Word Bank* ···

psyche	psychology	amnesia	memorandum
psychic	amnesty	commemorate	memorial

III. Define It! (Part 2)

DIRECTIONS: Based on what you have learned in this chapter, define each of the following in your own words, and create a sentence using the word.

1. psyche: _____

_____

2. psychic: _____

_____

3. psychology: _____

_____

4. amnesty: _____

_____

5. amnesia: _____

_____

6. commemorate: _____

_____

7. memorandum: _____

_____

8. memorial: _____

_____

IV. Personalize It!

DIRECTIONS: Using your understanding of the vocabulary words, respond to the following prompts. Use a separate piece of paper if necessary.

1. Describe something that you would like to *commemorate*.

_____

2. The United States is full of monuments that serve as *memorials* to people and events. Which *memorial* is the most significant to you and why?

_____

3. What would you do if you found you had *psychic* abilities?

_____

4. Are there any crimes that you believe people should receive *amnesty* for? Explain your opinion.

_____

Word Bank

psyche	psychology	amnesia	memorandum
psychic	amnesty	commemorate	memorial

V. Decode It!

DIRECTIONS: Use what you have learned about the roots *psych*, *mnem*, and *memor* and the suffixes you have learned to answer the following questions:

1. Remember that the suffix *–able* means "being capable of." What do we mean when we say something is *memorable*?

   _____

   _____

2. Sometimes athletes say they want to "psych out" their opponents by doing things that confuse them or instill fear in them. What does the word *psych* mean in this context?

   _____

   _____

3. The Latin root *memor* means "remembering." A *memoir* is a specific form of writing. What do you think a *memoir* describes?

   _____

   _____

4. A *mnemonic* device is a way of remembering information. In one type of *mnemonic* device, each word stands for something else. For example, "Every Good Boy Deserves Fudge" stands for the musical notes (E, G, B, D, F) on the lines of a treble clef. What is the root of *mnemonic*, and what is the relationship between the word and its root?

   _____

   _____

Chapter 18:
Exercises

··· *Word Bank* ···

psyche   psychology   amnesia   memorandum
psychic   amnesty   commemorate   memorial

VI. Put It In Context!

DIRECTIONS: Complete the sentence in a way that shows you understand what the vocabulary word in italics means.

1. A child's *psyche* may be damaged if…

_____

_____

2. Heather believed that she had *psychic* powers because…

_____

_____

3. Peter wanted to study *psychology* because…

_____

_____

4. The government offered *amnesty* to the spy because…

_____

_____

5. While Derek had *amnesia*…

_____

_____

6. At graduation, the choir sang a song to *commemorate*…

_____

_____

7. The boss's *memorandum* to the workers …

_____

_____

8. The city planted a tree as a *memorial* to…

_____

_____

Growing Your Vocabulary: Learning from Latin and Greek Roots

·········· *Word Bank* ··········

psyche	psychology	amnesia	memorandum
psychic	amnesty	commemorate	memorial

VII. Analogies!

DIRECTIONS: For each of the vocabulary words in the chapter, complete the analogy.

1. *Verdict* is to *jury* as _____ is to *government.*

2. *Love* is to *the* _____ as *nutrition* is to *the body.*

3. *Paper* is to a *memorandum* as a *statue* is to a _____.

4. _____ is to *unaware* as *awake* is to *asleep.*

5. _____ is to *the mind* as *cardiology* is to *the heart.*

6. *Memory* is to _____ as *flood* is to *drought.*

7. *Celebrate* is to _____ as *party* is to *memorial.*

8. *Boss* is to _____ as *boyfriend* is to *love letter.*

Word Bank

psyche	psychology	amnesia	memorandum
psychic	amnesty	commemorate	memorial

VIII. Write About It!

DIRECTIONS: In this chapter, you have learned words about the mind and memories. As a class, create a list of the prefixes, suffixes, and roots that you have trouble remembering. Then, create a *mnemonic* device that will help you remember the meanings. A *mnemonic* device is anything that will help you remember, so you may want to include art or music as well.

_____

_____

_____

_____

_____

_____

_____

_____

_____

Savvy

Option

Recognize   Connoisseur

Cognitive   Savor

Adopt   Opt

Cognizant

Incognito

Growing Your Vocabulary: Learning from Latin and Greek Roots

sav

opt

cogn

Chapter 19:
Better Choices through Knowledge

Did you know that having a college education will earn you almost $25,000 more a year than having only a high school education? Knowledge is power! In this chapter, you will learn vocabulary words that are related to knowledge.

Roots to Learn:
sav   opt
cogn

Words to Learn:	
savvy	connoisseur
savor	cognizant
recognize	opt
incognito	option
cognitive	adopt

The Latin word **SAPERE**, **SAPITUM** means both "to taste" and "to be aware or to think." The root **SAV** comes from this word even though it looks slightly different.

SAVVY means "knowledgeable or clever."

SAVOR means "to continue to taste" by holding in the mouth or mind.

*The **savvy** skiers know which hills to head for and which to avoid.*

Did You Know?

How is it that words from *sapere, sapitum* mean both "to taste" and "to think"? The Latin verb *sapere, sapitum* originally meant "to taste." Gradually, it also came to mean "perceive differences in taste," and then "to perceive, to understand." That's why we get words like *savor*, which pertains to taste, and *sapient*, which has to do with thinking, from this Latin word. We also, by the way, get the word *insipid*, a synonym for "boring," which literally means "having no flavor."

Chapter 19:
Better Choices through Knowledge

The Latin verb **COGNOSCERE**, **COGNITUM** means "to know." Words that come from its root **COGN** relate to mental perception.

To **RECOGNIZE** means "to see something that you've seen before."

Dogs rely on their noses to **RECOGNIZE** one another. Bees use other bees' dancing to do the same. Ants recognize where food is because they can communicate through touching their antennas. So, while the word *recognize* has the root *cogn* in it, the word doesn't always deal with knowing through intelligence. Nature has made all animals able to recognize what they need by many techniques.

*Maria's friends said they barely **recognized** her with her hair dyed a different color.*

*The famous actor found that he could walk the city streets **incognito** if he wore a hat and sunglasses.*

INCOGNITO means "in disguise."

When is everyone **INCOGNITO**? On Halloween, of course! Everybody is pretending to be someone or something they are not. An interesting fact about this scary holiday is that it was brought to America by Irish immigrants, who believed that October 31st was a day on which the boundary between life and death dissolved, so people would wear masks to confuse returning spirits. Sound close enough to what we do on Halloween nowadays? Trick or treating began as a way to make the dead spirits happy, by giving them treats.

COGNITIVE means "having to do with thought and thinking."

Look at the cartoon. It seems impossible that someone that young could do math! And it probably is. But many people have developed **COGNITIVE** abilities that are quite amazing. A famous British philosopher named John Stuart Mill learned Greek by the time he was three, and he learned Latin by age ten. Supposedly, Mill's I. Q. was over 200.

*April's **cognitive** abilities are very advanced for a child her age.*

Growing Your Vocabulary: Learning from Latin and Greek Roots

A **CONNOISSEUR** is someone with advanced knowledge in a specific area.

There are automobile **CONNOISSEURS**, wine connoisseurs, cigar and coffee connoisseurs, clothing, jewelry, plant, music, airplane, and perfume connoisseurs, and probably connoisseurs of millions of different topics. Sometimes, a person who is a connoisseur would be called a "snob" or "stuck up" by other people, whose knowledge of a certain subject is not as advanced.

*Ms. Jiminez is a **connoisseur** of fine cheeses.*

*Vernon became **cognizant** of many changes in the town.*

COGNIZANT means "being aware."

In this chapter, you've seen the word *recognize*, and now you come upon **COGNIZANT**. Both of them seem very similar in meaning. But they are different! Suppose you're at the zoo and you go into the big cat house to look at the carnivorous animals. You will, obviously, recognize lions, tigers, maybe a leopard, but you may not be cognizant of how they live, what kinds of meat they eat, or their enemies. You can see by this explanation that the two words really do have different meanings.

Chapter 19:
Better Choices through Knowledge

The Latin verb **OPTARE**, **OPTATUM** means "to choose." This word gives us the root **OPT**.

OPT means "to choose."

You probably have heard, read, or studied many words that have *opt* in them—words like *optimism* (a positive outlook), *optometrist* (an eye doctor), or *optimum* (the best). However, none of them relate to this one word, *opt*. You will simply have to rely on your *optic* nerve and your memory to determine the differences among all the *opt* words you encounter.

*Nilan **opted** to walk to work instead of taking the bus today.*

*There are several vegetarian **options** on the menu.*

An **OPTION** is a choice.

Life is made up of **OPTIONS**. What clothes do you wear each morning? What cereal is your favorite? Who will you vote for in an election? What should you name the dog? Where would you go on a honeymoon? People are different from most other animals when it comes to choices. Wild animals have very few options because they are guided by instinct. A bird cannot decide whether to fly south for the winter, and a dog cannot decide if he should bark at a stranger or not. Aren't you glad you can make choices by using your rational brain?

ADOPT means "to choose for oneself."

Many children are **ADOPTED**—over 120,000 each year in the U. S. alone. Throughout the world, that number is much higher. What are some reasons for adopting a child? Some couples want children, but can't have any, some have medical reasons and cannot have any more children, some people adopt children with disabilities who otherwise would be forced to stay in hospitals, and still others adopt a relative's child if the birth parents cannot take care of the baby. Whatever the reason is, most parents love their adopted children just as much as children who are born into their family.

*Leslie always got the best scores on her tests, Ronald decided to **adopt** her method of study*

Growing Your Vocabulary: Learning from Latin and Greek Roots

Exercises
Word Bank

savvy	savor	incognito	connoisseur	option
cognizant	recognize	cognitive	opt	adopt

I. Define It! (Part 1)

DIRECTIONS: Write the letter of the word from the right column that matches the definition in the left column. The first one has been done for you.

1. to choose **D**
2. in disguise ___
3. to continue to taste; to keep in the mouth or mind ___
4. a choice ___
5. having to do with thought and thinking ___
6. someone with a great deal of knowledge in a specific area ___
7. to choose for oneself ___
8. aware ___
9. knowledgeable; clever ___
10. to see something you've seen before ___

A. incognito
B. adopt
C. cognizant
D. opt
E. savvy
F. option
G. cognitive
H. connoisseur
I. recognize
J. savor

II. Finish It!

DIRECTIONS: Using the root, write a word to complete each sentence. The first one has been done for you.

1. Some scientific studies show that _____**cognitive**_____ ability begins to decline as a person reaches middle age. (Root = COGN)
2. Because of the numerous classes that Stephen had taken on precious stones, he could be considered a(n) _____ of fine jewelry. (Root = COGN)
3. Bruce was so _____ when writing his poem about Michael Jordan that he was able to write it in the shape of Jordan himself. (Root = SAV)
4. At lunch, the students had the _____ of choosing a pepperoni pizza or a chicken sandwich. (Root = OPT)
5. Cassie barely _____ her best friend after he got his hair cut. (Root = COGN)
6. Many celebrities wear disguises so they can walk around _____. (Root = COGN)
7. The local junior high school _____ a French bulldog as its mascot. (Root = OPT)
8. Sandy _____ the taste of the turkey that her mother cooked only once a year. (Root = SAV)
9. When Bob bought his new truck, he _____ to buy "green" and purchased the hybrid truck rather than the one with the bigger engine. (Root = OPT)
10. Tanya's speech went very well until she became _____ of how many people in the audience were staring at her. (Root = COGN)

······· *Word Bank* ·······

savvy	savor	incognito	connoisseur	option
cognizant	recognize	cognitive	opt	adopt

III. Define It! (Part 2)

DIRECTIONS: Based on what you have learned in this chapter, define each of the following in your own words, and create a sentence using the word.

1. recognize: _____

_____

2. cognitive: _____

_____

3. incognito: _____

_____

4. cognizant: _____

_____

5. connoisseur: _____

_____

6. savor: _____

_____

7. savvy: _____

_____

8. opt: _____

_____

9. option: _____

_____

10. adopt: _____

_____

·· *Word Bank* ··

savvy   savor   incognito   connoisseur   option
cognizant   recognize   cognitive   opt   adopt

IV. Personalize It!

DIRECTIONS: Using your understanding of the vocabulary words, respond to the following prompts. Use a separate piece of paper if necessary.

1. A *connoisseur* is an expert in a specific field. In what field are you or would you like to be a *connoisseur*? Why?

   _____

   _____

2. If you wanted to be *incognito* for a while, what would your disguise be?

   _____

   _____

3. As you continue to mature, you will be able to *adopt* habits that will help you be the best student you can be. What type of habits should a person *adopt* that will enable him or her to be successful in school?

   _____

   _____

4. Describe a few *options* that you would like to have available at lunch.

   _____

   _____

·············· Word Bank ··············

savvy	savor	incognito	connoisseur	option
cognizant	recognize	cognitive	opt	adopt

V. Unscramble It!

DIRECTIONS: The vocabulary words from the chapter have been scrambled. Using the sentence, figure out which word belongs in the blank. Then, unscramble the letters to write the word correctly.

1. The _____ salesman knew exactly how to convince people to buy his useless junk.
   VAYSV

2. The teacher told her class that they had the _____ of using either pen or pencil.
   TONPIO

3. The parents of the first-grader who could read an encyclopedia thought her _____ ability came from being read to every night before bed.
   TECINGOIV

4. The _____ of chocolate could list the ingredients of any candy bar after tasting it once.
   ESOSUNCROIN

5. At the animal shelter, my sister and I decided to _____ two kittens from the same litter.
   ODPAT

6. I wore a wig and glasses to the party so I would be _____.
   NGOTICNIO

7. Blake's family _____ to spend their summer vacation at home to save money.
   OTEDP

8. We had not seen our cousins in such a long time that it was difficult to _____ them.
   EORCNZGIE

9. Thanksgiving dinner was so tasty that I wanted to _____ every bite.
   OVARS

10. The mountain frequently has falling rocks and avalanches, so climbers must always be _____ of their environment.
    NAGOTCZIN

.... *Word Bank* ....

savvy	savor	incognito	connoisseur	option
cognizant	recognize	cognitive	opt	adopt

VI. Compare It! (Synonyms)

DIRECTIONS: The words in this chapter have synonyms that will help you learn the meaning of the vocabulary words. Match each vocabulary word with a word that means something similar to it.

1. conscious **C**
2. accept ____
3. crafty ____
4. identify ____
5. appreciate ____
6. thinking ____
7. select ____
8. concealed ____
9. expert ____
10. alternative ____

A. option
B. adopt
C. cognizant
D. opt
E. savvy
F. incognito
G. cognitive
H. connoisseur
I. recognize
J. savor

VII. Compare It! (Antonyms and Synonyms)

DIRECTIONS: Some words in this chapter have antonyms or synonyms that will help you learn their meanings. Match the clues in the left column with a synonym from the right column and then match the rest of the clues with their antonyms.

Synonym:
1. identify ____
2. thinking ____
3. aware ____
4. selection ____
5. enjoy ____
6. elect ____

Antonym:
7. reject ____
8. know-nothing ____
9. recognizable ____
10. foolish ____

Original:
A. option
B. adopt
C. cognizant
D. opt
E. savvy
F. incognito
G. cognitive
H. connoisseur
I. recognize
J. savor

Word Bank

savvy	savor	incognito	connoisseur	option
cognizant	recognize	cognitive	opt	adopt

VIII. Put It In Context!

DIRECTIONS: Complete the sentence in a way that shows you understand what the vocabulary word in *italics* means.

1. I thought I saw my cousin on the bus, but it was hard to *recognize* him because…

_____

_____

2. Jeff put his *cognitive* skills to the test when…

_____

_____

3. Police officers sometimes need to go *incognito* when…

_____

_____

4. The airline pilot must be *cognizant* of…

_____

_____

5. The food *connoisseur* impressed everyone when…

_____

_____

6. The gardener likes to *savor*…

_____

_____

7. Week after week, the *savvy* weather reporter gave people…

_____

_____

8. The students *opted* to go to the theatre and…

_____

_____

9. You have the *option* of taking public transportation if…

_____

_____

10. When my family *adopted* the puppy, they…

_____

_____

·· *Word Bank* ··

| savvy | savor | incognito | connoisseur | option |
| cognizant | recognize | cognitive | opt | adopt |

IX. Write About It!

DIRECTIONS: In this chapter, you have learned words about knowledge and choices. Explain the meaning of the following quote: "The pen is mightier than the sword." Try to use at least three of the vocabulary words in your explanation.

_____

_____

_____

_____

_____

_____

_____

_____

_____

Belligerent

Pacify

Pact

Placate

Placid

Rebel

Placebo

Bellicose

Growing Your Vocabulary: Learning from Latin and Greek Roots

bell

plac

pac

Chapter 20:
War and Peace

The United States has been involved in two major world wars and many other military combats. Can you name five of them besides World War I and World War II? This chapter will introduce you to words that deal with war and peace.

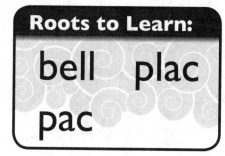

Roots to Learn:

bell **plac**

pac

Words to Learn:

bellicose	pact
belligerent	placid
rebel	placebo
pacify	placate

Let's start with the Latin words for "war" and "peace": **BELLUS** (war) and **PAX**, **PACIS** (peace). The roots **BELL** and **PAC** come from these words.

BELLICOSE means "eager to fight."

Sometimes sports fans can be extremely **BELLICOSE** during a game between teams that have been rivals for a long time, such as the Boston Red Sox and the New York Yankees. Fans might yell insults at the players, throw things, or even get out of their seats to try to get on the field. Don't these bellicose fans know that it's just a game?

*The **bellicose** young man was ready to fight with anyone. Mr. Jenkins decided it was time to talk about his attitude.*

Chapter 20:
War and Peace

BELLIGERENT means "warlike or hostile."

Before World War II began, Germany acted **BELLIGERENTLY** against other European countries. First, Germany invaded Poland and conquered it. Adolph Hitler, Germany's leader, agreed to not invade any more territory (he was still bellicose, however), but less than two years later, Germany's belligerent behavior erupted again, and it invaded Denmark, a few other countries, and then France. Fortunately, England and the United States remained out of Hitler's grip, and the Nazi army was defeated in 1945.

*Oliver dreaded seeing the **belligerent** customer who came into his restaurant every day.*

To **REBEL** means "to rise in opposition."

During the Civil War, the soldiers who fought in the southern states were called "Rebels." This isn't because they were soldiers who rebelled against their commanders, but because they rebelled against the Union. Many states seceded from, or left, the United States to become part of the Confederate States of America. You can still see some of these ideas in rebellious statements such as "Don't mess with Texas."

*No one expected the soldiers in the platoon to **rebel** against their leader.*

Growing Your Vocabulary: Learning from Latin and Greek Roots

The Latin word **PAX**, **PACIS** means "peace." The root **PAC** comes from this word.

To **PACIFY** means "to make peace."

Did You Know?

A person who believes that fighting is not the way to resolve disputes is called a *pacifist*. There have been many of these pacifists throughout history, and many of them died or were murdered for their cause. Think of Mahatma Gandhi or Martin Luther King, Jr. One *pacifist* who did not die because of his beliefs is Nelson Mandela. He didn't begin his struggle as a believer in nonviolence, but he became one while he was in prison in South Africa for over 27 years.

*Priya's attempt to **pacify** the cat made it more angry.*

*Clint and Antoine made a **pact** and were friends forever.*

A **PACT** is an agreement, often one for peace.

You might think that a **PACT** is similar to a "contract." You'd be right—almost. However, there are important differences. All contracts are legal documents, but most pacts are not. Soldiers often make pacts before a battle, people make pacts among themselves, and you might even have a pact with people from another neighborhood about something. None of these would be written down, and none would be considered legal arrangements. You need to remember this important difference.

Chapter 20:
War and Peace

The Latin word **PLACERE**, **PLACITUS** means "to make calm." The root from this verb is **PLAC**.

PLACID means "calm, smooth, or undisturbed."

In New York state, there's a lake called Lake Placid. What do you think it looks like? If you understand the meaning of the word, you'll know that the water is still and quiet, and that it does not contain any dangerous sea creatures. It's beautiful, peaceful, quiet, and calm.

*It's a sunny and **placid** spring day near the lake.*

*Some people received the actual test medication, while others were given a **placebo**.*

A **PLACEBO** is something that has no real effect or value, but seems to.

Many times a **PLACEBO** works as well as real medicine. That has led scientists to come up with a theory called the "placebo effect," which means that merely thinking that a certain medicine will help cure a disease or a pain will actually help cure it. The human brain is a powerful organ if it can do something as amazing as this!

To **PLACATE** means "to calm or pacify."

Recently, some parents in a school district were upset because their kids' test scores had fallen, but the school board wanted to increase all principals' salaries anyway. At a meeting of the PTA, many parents became bellicose (remember that word?) and demanded that the school board change their decision. In an effort to **PLACATE** them, the board voted to increase the budget and spend more on books and teachers' salaries instead. It worked, and the schools in that district have improved ever since.

*Brianna tried to **placate** her sister by promising her a trip to the playground.*

Growing Your Vocabulary: Learning from Latin and Greek Roots

Exercises
Word Bank

belligerent	rebel	pact	placebo
bellicose	pacify	placid	placate

I. Define It! (Part 1)

DIRECTIONS: Write the letter of the word from the right column that matches the definition in the left column. The first one has been done for you.

1. to make peaceful **C**

2. a peace agreement ___

3. a drug that has no real effect, but seems to cause improvement ___

4. eager to fight ___

5. calm; smooth; undisturbed ___

6. warlike or hostile ___

7. to calm; to pacify ___

8. to rise in opposition ___

A. placate

B. pact

C. pacify

D. belligerent

E. bellicose

F. placid

G. rebel

H. placebo

II. Finish It!

DIRECTIONS: Using the root provided, write a word to complete each sentence.
The first one has been done for you.

1. When the principal changed the school's start time to 5:45 A.M., parents, teachers, and students decided to _____**rebel**_____ and called the school to complain. (Root = BELL)

2. The _____ water that glimmered like a sheet of ice-blue glass slowly put the cruise passengers to sleep. (Root = PLAC)

3. Cory's _____ attitude and angry face earned him detention when the teacher tried to correct his behavior. (Root = BELL)

4. Because the _____ seemed to cure the patient, the doctor knew that Sondar's illness was not completely physical. (Root = PLAC)

5. The _____ girl seemed to pick a fight with anyone who made eye contact with her. (Root = BELL)

6. The restaurant manager attempted to _____ unhappy customers by offering them discount coupons for their next visit. (Root = PLAC)

7. Under the conditions of the peace _____, the two nations would assist one another in defense. (Root = PAC)

8. The mother tried to _____ her crying baby by offering her a bottle. (Root = PAC)

.... Word Bank ....

| belligerent | rebel | pact | placebo |
| bellicose | pacify | placid | placate |

III. Define It! (Part 2)

DIRECTIONS: Based on what you have learned in this chapter, define each of the following in your own words, and create a sentence using the word.

1. belligerent: _____

_____

2. bellicose: _____

_____

3. rebel: _____

_____

4. pacify: _____

_____

5. pact: _____

_____

6. placid: _____

_____

7. placebo: _____

_____

8. placate: _____

_____

IV. Analogies!

DIRECTIONS: For each of the vocabulary words in the chapter, complete the analogy.

1. *Agree* is to _____ as *anger* is to *friendship*.

2. A *handshake* is to a _____ as a *signature* is to a *contract*.

3. _____ is to *troublemaker* as *agreeable* is to *good citizen*.

4. *Dangerous* is to *poison* as *harmless* is to _____.

5. *Rough* is to *calm* as *hostile* is to _____.

6. _____ is to *warlike* as *gentle* is to *easygoing*.

7. *Calm* is to _____ as *angry* is to *enrage*.

8. *Bother* is to *annoy* as *soothe* is to _____.

······· *Word Bank* ·······

| belligerent | rebel | pact | placebo |
| bellicose | pacify | placid | placate |

V. Apply It To The Real World!

DIRECTIONS: You have learned the basic definitions of the words in this chapter. You have even had the opportunity to use the words in sentences; however, you should also know how they are applied in the real world. Choose the vocabulary word that best answers each of the following questions:

1. Which vocabulary word describes someone who is angry and ready to fight _____

2. Which vocabulary word describes a warm, pleasant day? _____

3. Which vocabulary word describes a harmless substance that could be used in a medical experiment? _____

4. Which vocabulary word describes a person who goes out of his way to start a fight? _____

5. Which vocabulary word describes what the Continental Army did in the Revolutionary War? _____

6. Which vocabulary word describes what people make when they are trying to resolve a fight? _____

VI. Find It!

DIRECTIONS: You have been introduced to eight vocabulary words that are formed from the roots *bell, pac,* and *plac*. However, there are many more words in the English language that use these roots. Using a dictionary, find the definition for the following words that are derived from these roots. Some words have more than one definition, but you should choose the definition that relates most directly to the theme of the chapter.

1. pacific:

_____

2. rebellion:

_____

3. appease:

_____

4. pacification:

_____

5. complacent:

_____

VII. Solve It!

DIRECTIONS: Use the clues and words from this chapter to complete the crossword puzzle. Some of the words may be in a different part of speech.

Word Bank

- belligerent
- bellicose
- rebel
- pacify
- pact
- placid
- placebo
- placate

Clues:

ACROSS

4. This word can be used as a synonym for *pacify*.

5. Sailing is best when the ocean is like this.

7. Researchers studying the effects of a drug may use this to control their study.

8. If you act in this manner, you are likely to start a fight.

DOWN

1. An infant may suck his or her thumb for this purpose.

2. People who strongly disagree with rules may do this.

3. This word can be used as a synonym for *belligerent*.

6. A contract is another form of this.

Unscramble the letters in the circles in the crossword puzzle to make a word that fits in the blanks in the sentence below. The unscrambled word is not one of the vocabulary words from this lesson, but it is related to some of them.

During the Civil War, the South started a ___ ___ ___ ___ ___ ___ ___ ___ against the North.

| belligerent | rebel | pact | placebo |
| bellicose | pacify | placid | placate |

VIII. Write About It!

DIRECTIONS: In this chapter, you have learned words about war and peace. It may be difficult for some of you to recall periods of war and peace our country has gone through, but you may remember periods of hostility or anger and periods of calm and peacefulness in your own lives. Write a poem that describes a time that hostility (maybe a war, a family disagreement, or something similar) has affected you, or write a poem about a time when you have felt completely at peace.

_____

_____

_____

_____

_____

_____

_____

_____

_____

_____

Review It!

DIRECTIONS: Read each question. Then, circle the letter next to the best answer.

1. A word meaning "rise up against" is
    A. savor.
    B. rebel.
    C. pacify.
    D. recognize.
    E. verify.

2. Which of the following words has to do with reason?
    A. pact
    B. infidel
    C. belligerent
    D. rational
    E. placate

3. An antonym for *pacify* is
    A. run.
    B. calm.
    C. recognize.
    D. confide.
    E. upset.

4. The Latin root in the word *sequel* means
    A. to follow.
    B. to understand.
    C. to calm down.
    D. to wage war.
    E. to forget.

5. The Latin word meaning "truth" gives us the word
    A. option.
    B. verify.
    C. ratio.
    D. savvy.
    E. memorandum.

6. The study of the human mind is called
    A. rationale.
    B. psychology.
    C. amnesty.
    D. veracity.
    E. pacify.

Review It!

7. Choose the word that best completes the sentence below:

Dan was afraid to _____ in Iyana because he knew that she was terrible at keeping secrets.

   A. confide
   B. recognize
   C. verify
   D. pacify
   E. opt

8. The Latin root meaning "calm" appears in the word
   A. placate.
   B. amnesty.
   C. fidelity.
   D. opt.
   E. verify.

9. Someone who is not faithful is a(n)
   A. option.
   B. memorial.
   C. amnesia.
   D. sequel.
   E. infidel.

10. The word *ratio* comes from the Latin word meaning
   A. truth.
   B. memory.
   C. war.
   D. reason.
   E. peace.

11. Choose the word that best completes the sentence below:

John dedicated the garden as a _____ to his friend.
   A. ratio
   B. memorandum
   C. memorial
   D. consequence
   E. verdict

12. Which of the following would be given by a jury?
   A. savvy
   B. verdict
   C. consequence
   D. amnesty
   E. psychology

Growing Your Vocabulary: Learning from Latin and Greek Roots

Review It!

13. Which word is a synonym for *choice*?
    A. option
    B. ration
    C. amnesia
    D. fidelity
    E. placebo

14. The Latin prefix meaning "not" appears in the word
    A. confide.
    B. adopt.
    C. recognize.
    D. subsequent.
    E. incognito.

15. The root *seq* in the word *subsequent* comes from the Latin word meaning
    A. to know.
    B. to remember.
    C. to follow.
    D. to forgive.
    E. to choose.

16. Which word below means the same thing as *clever*?
    A. cognizant
    B. incognito
    C. savvy
    D. placid
    E. belligerent

17. Choose the word that best completes the sentence below:

    I didn't recognize you; are you _____ today?

    A. incognito
    B. savvy
    C. placid
    D. rational
    E. bellicose

18. The word *opt* comes from the Latin word meaning
    A. to forget.
    B. to wage war.
    C. to follow.
    D. to choose.
    E. to trust.

Review It!

19. Which word means the opposite of *cause*?
    A. pact
    B. consequence
    C. placebo
    D. savor
    E. psyche

20. Which of the following words has to do with thinking?
    A. cognitive
    B. placid
    C. subsequent
    D. memorial
    E. belligerent

21. A measurement of proportion is a
    A. connoisseur.
    B. ratio.
    C. confidant.
    D. pact.
    E. veracity.

22. Another word for "loss of memory" is
    A. psyche.
    B. memorandum.
    C. amnesia.
    D. placebo.
    E. sequence.

23. Choose the word that best completes the sentence below:

    That large monument was erected to _____ the Battle of Gettysburg.

    A. savor
    B. commemorate
    C. adopt
    D. placate
    E. confide

24. The word *cognizant* means
    A. skillful.
    B. calm.
    C. forgetful.
    D. warlike.
    E. aware.

Words to Learn

Chapter 1

gene	progeny	genre
congenital	generate	generic

Chapter 2

survive	vivid	mortal	mortify
revive	vivacious	immortal ·	morbid

Chapter 3

cardiologist	epidermis	anemia	prenatal
cardiovascular	dermatology	hemorrhage	neonatal

Chapter 4

luminous	illuminate	elucidate	photosynthesis
luminary	lucid	photon	

Chapter 5

projectile	interject	mobile	remove	motive
eject	dejected	immobile ·	remote	motivate

Chapter 6

grave	aggravate	pendant	pending
gravitate	pendulum	appendix	pensive

Chapter 7

levity	alleviate	lever	altitude
elevate	levitate	relieve	exalt

Chapter 8

capture	captivate	except	anticipate	participate
captive	accept	intercept	recipient	

Chapter 9

inter	tenant	tenure	trite
subterranean	tenement	continent	attrition

Chapter 10

homo sapiens	anthropology	philanthropy
homicide	misanthrope	android

Chapter 11

artisan	artifice	ornate	apt	adept
artificial	adorn	adapt	aptitude	inept

Chapter 12

dictate	diction	contradict	monologue
indict	edict	dialogue	prologue

Chapter 13

arrogant	interrogate	acquire	inquisitive
prerogative	query	inquisition	quest

Chapter 14

monarch	potent	potential	omnipotent
anarchy	impotent	potentate	

Chapter 15

legislate	justice	jurisdiction	jurisprudence
legitimate	justify	perjure	

Chapter 16

verify	verdict	infidel	confidant
veracity	fidelity	confide	

Chapter 17

sequence	consequence	ratio	rational
sequel	subsequent	ration	rationale

Chapter 18

psyche	psychology	amnesia	memorandum
psychic	amnesty	commemorate	memorial

Chapter 19

savvy	recognize	cognitive	cognizant	option
savor	incognito	connoisseur	opt	adopt

Chapter 20

bellicose	rebel	pact	placebo
belligerent	pacify	placid	placate

Roots and Affixes

Chapter 1
gen
gener
pro–
–al
–ic/ics
–ate

Chapter 2
viv
mort/mor
re–
im–
–ious
–ify

Chapter 3
card
derm
hem/em
nat
cardio–
epi–
a–
pre–
neo–
–ar
–logy
–ist

Chapter 4
lumin
luc
phot
–er

Chapter 5
ject
mob
mot/mov
e–
inter–
de–

Chapter 6
grav
pend/pens
–ant
–ive

Chapter 7
lev
alt
–y

Chapter 8
capt
cept
cip

Chapter 9
ter
ten/tin
trit
sub–
con–

Chapter 10
hom
anthropo
andro
mis–
–cide

Chapter 11
art
orn
apt/ept
–ial

Chapter 12
dict
log
mono–
dia–

Chapter 13
roga
quer/quisit

Chapter 14
arch
pot
omni–

Chapter 15
leg
jus/jur
–ice

Chapter 16
ver
fid

Chapter 17
sequ
rat

Chapter 18
psych
mnem
memor

Chapter 19
sav
cogn
opt

Chapter 20
bell
pac
plac

Growing Your Vocabulary: Learning from Latin and Greek Roots